GRAMMARWORK

2

English Exercises
in Context

PAMELA PETERSON BREYER

PRENTICE HALL REGENTS
A VIACOM COMPANY
Upper Saddle River, New Jersey 07458

Acquisitions Editor: Nancy Leonhardt
Management of Development Services: Louisa B. Hellegers
Development Editors: Carol Callahan and Penny La Porte

Direction of Production: Aliza Greenblatt
Editorial Production/Design Manager: Dominick Mosco

Production Coordinator: Ray Keating
Production Supervision/Page Composition: Noël Vreeland Carter
Art Director: Merle Krumper
Cover Design: Marianne Frasco
Electronic Art: Ken Liao
Interior design: Patrice Fodero
Interior Art: Lane Gregory and Dorothea Sierra

© 1996 by PRENTICE HALL REGENTS
Prentice-Hall Inc.
A Simon & Schuster Company
Upper Saddle River, New Jersey 07458

PRENTICE HALL REGENTS
A VIACOM COMPANY

Printed in the United States of America
10 9 8 7 6 5 4 3 2 1

ISBN 0-13-340258-4

Prentice-Hall International (UK) Limited, *London*
Prentice-Hall of Australia Pty. Limited, *Sydney*
Prentice-Hall of Canada Inc., *Toronto*
Prentice-Hall Hispanoamericana, S.A., *Mexico*
Prentice-Hall of India Private Limited, *New Delhi*
Prentice-Hall of Japan, Inc., *Tokyo*
Simon & Schuster Asia Pte. Ltd., *Singapore*
Editora Prentice-Hall do Brasil, Ltda., *Rio de Janeiro*

Printed on Recycle Paper

To my father, Loyl Peterson

CONTENTS

Present Continuous

Future with *Going To*

Future with *Will*

Simple Present

Comparisons

Imperatives and Requests

Modals and Idiomatic Modals

Simple Past

Past Continuous

Present Be + Past Participle

Recent studies have shown that students acquire and retain a new language more rapidly and more efficiently when the structure and vocabulary of the language are presented in context; that is, when elements of a lesson, such as grammar and new lexicon, are tied together in some real and meaningful setting. Exercises that present material in such a situational context are referred to as contextualized exercises.

GrammarWork is a series of four contextualized exercise books for students of written English. These books may be used as major texts or as supplementary material, depending on whether a course is nonintensive or intensive. Each exercise in each book presents, as a unit, vocabulary relating to a particular context and structures that are appropriate to that context.

Book One is intended for the beginner: the student enrolled in a first-level English course who has had some exposure to the language. Book Two continues with beginners' material, proceeding from first-level to second-level work. Book Three is designed for the intermediate student, and Book Four contains material appropriate to high-intermediate levels.

The books are organized into grammatical units (i.e., the Verb *To Be*, the Present Continuous, the Simple Present). Each unit contains a variety of exercises with practice in small increments. Most units include more than one exercise on key grammar points, in order to give students sufficient and varied practice. Also included in each unit are review exercises and periodic tense contrast exercises, usually located at the end of the unit.

The pages in each book are, for the most part, divided into three sections:

a. an examination of the structure to be presented (**Grammar**);

b. exercises that enable the student to manipulate that new structure in a contextual setting (**Practice**); and

c. a culminating exercise activity in which the student uses the material in the exercise by applying it to some personal, real-life situation (**Make It Work**).

The **Grammar** section shows the student how to use the structure to be practiced, with diagrams and arrows that should be self-explanatory. Notes of explanation are supplied only when the grammar rule cannot be illustrated clearly.

The **Practice** section consists of a contextualized exercise, usually a page in length and always self-contained; if a context is three pages instead of one, the will be self-contained within those three pages. Thus the teacher can select any exercise or group of exercises he or she considers appropriate for a particular class, lesson, or given time. The teacher can choose to utilize all the exercises in the order presented. The exercises have been arranged in ascending order of difficulty, with structures generally considered to be the easiest for most students presented first.

The exercises are self-contained in that they have been designed for written practice without necessarily being preceded by an introductory teacher's presentation. Since grammatical diagrams have been included and the new vocabulary is usually illustrated or defined, students can work independently, either at home or in class—in pairs or as a group. When students work together in pairs or in groups in the classroom, they should be encouraged to help each other; the teacher, too, can assist by circulating from pair to pair or group to group, guiding and correcting.

The **Make It Work** section enables students to apply what they have been practicing to freer, and sometimes more natural, situations. The activity usually contains a picture cue, a fill-in dialogue, or questions to answer. The purpose of the **Make It Work** section is to provide the student with as real-life a setting as possible.

The perforated answer key can be used by either the student or the teacher. The teacher may choose to withhold the answers on some occasions; on other occasions, the students may use the answer key for self-correction.

MADONNA ISN'T JUST A SINGER. SHE'S ALSO AN ACTRESS.

Negative and Affirmative Statements: Contracted Forms
Verb *To Be*

S - Madonna | isn't | just a singer. *He's* | She's | also an actress.
P - Madonna and Cher | aren't | just singers. | They're | also actresses.

contractions: isn't = is not   aren't = are not   's = is   're = are

P R A C T I C E

Fill in the blanks with *isn't* or *aren't*. Then make sentences with pronouns and contractions.

1. Paula Abdul _____*isn't*_____ just a singer. _____*She's*_____ also a dancer.

2. Barbra Streisand and Cher _____ just singers. _____ also actresses.

3. Paul Newman _____ just an actor. _____ also a race car driver.

4. Bill Cosby and Eddie Murphy _____ just comedians. _____ also actors.

5. Shirley MacLaine _____ just an actress. _____ also a writer.

6. Kevin Costner and Clint Eastwood _____ just actors. _____ also movie directors.

7. Elizabeth Taylor _____ just an actress. _____ also a businessperson.

8. Liza Minnelli and Madonna _____ just singers. _____ also actresses.

9. John McEnroe _____ just a tennis player. _____ also a sportscaster.

10. Oprah Winfrey _____ just a talk show host. _____ also an actress.

11. Deion Sanders and Bo Jackson _____ just baseball players. _____ also football players.

12. Lee Iacocca _____ just a businessperson. _____ also a writer.

MAKE IT WORK

Tell about someone who has two occupations.

_____ just _____.

_____ also a _____.

1

WHOSE UMBRELLA IS IT?

Questions with *Whose*

Verb *To Be*

> This isn't my umbrella.
> | Whose | umbrella is it? ~ S
>
> These aren't my glasses.
> | Whose | glasses are they? ~ P

PRACTICE

Make questions with *whose.*

1. This isn't my umbrella.   _Whose umbrella is it?_
2. These aren't my gloves. ~ P   _____
3. This isn't my wallet. ~ S   _____
4. These aren't my keys. ~   _Whose keys are they_
5. These aren't my books. ~   _Whose books are they_
6. This isn't my scarf. ~ S   _Whose scarf is it_
7. These aren't my credit cards.   _Whose credit cards are_
8. These aren't my pens. ~   _Whose pens are they_
9. This isn't my camera. ~   _Whose camera is it_
10. These aren't my pencils.   _Whose pencils are they_
11. This isn't my coat. ~ S   _Whose coat is it_
12. These aren't my papers.   _Whose papers_
13. This isn't my purse. ~   _Whose purse_
14. This isn't my hat. ~   _Whose_

MAKE IT WORK

Look at the dialogue. Then write a dialogue about glasses.

■ Is this your camera?	■ _____
☐ No, it isn't.	☐ _____
■ Then whose camera is it?	■ _____
☐ I don't know.	☐ _____

2

IT'S MR. JONES'S PEN.

Possessive of Singular Nouns
Verb *To Be*

Whose pen is this?		Mr. Jones ['s]	
	It's		pen.
		the waitress ['s]	
Whose pens are these?		John Goode ['s]	
	They're		pens.
		the secretary ['s]	

Note: Add **'s** to form the possessive.

P R A C T I C E

Answer the questions. Use the words in parentheses ( ).

1. Whose umbrella is this? (Chris)   *It's Chris's umbrella.* _____

2. Whose pencil is this? (the waitress) _____

3. Whose keys are these? (Gloria) _____

4. Whose wallet is this? (Robert) _____

5. Whose office is this? (the boss) _____

6. Whose scarf is this? (Anita) _____

7. Whose sunglasses are these?
   (Mark Gunn) _____

8. Whose gloves are these?
   (Dr. Adams) _____

9. Whose camera is this? (John Goode) _____

10. Whose books are these? (Mr. Jones) _____

11. Whose glasses are these? (Dr. Bittel) _____

12. Whose business card is this?
    (Brian Burns) _____

13. Whose coat is this? (Charles) _____

14. Whose papers are these? (Dr. Morgan) _____

Ordinal Numbers

Verb *To Be*

first	(1st)	sixth	(6th)
second	(2nd)	seventh	(7th)
third	(3rd)	eighth	(8th)
fourth	(4th)	ninth	(9th)
fifth	(5th)	tenth	(10th)

Where are the elevators?   They're on the first floor.

Where's Thanos's Coffee Shop?   It's on the tenth floor.

① The Towers Building Directory ①

10th floor	Thanos's Coffee Shop **Restrooms**
9th floor	John B. Goode, Photographer
8th floor	Mark Gunn, Detective
7th floor	Anita Hug And Gloria Sanchez, Interior Decorators
6th floor	Chris Green And Brian Burns, Real Estate Agents
5th floor	*****Five Star Employment Agency*****
4th floor	Art Jones, Attorney At Law
3rd floor	Charles Bittel, Optometrist
2nd floor	Robert Morgan, M.D. Samuel Adams, M.D.

1st floor	Telephones	Mailboxes	Vending Machines	Elevators

New Words: attorney = lawyer

optometrist = eye doctor

M.D. = medical doctor

THEY'RE ON THE FIRST FLOOR.

PRACTICE

Look at the directory on page 4. Then answer the questions.

1. Where are the telephones? *They're on the first floor.*
2. Where's Dr. Morgan's office? _____
3. Where's Thanos's Coffee Shop? _____
4. Where are the mailboxes? _____
5. Where's Five Star Employment Agency? _____
   _____
6. Where's Gloria Sanchez's office? _____
7. Where are the restrooms? _____
8. Where's Charles Bittel's office? _____
9. Where's Mark Gunn's office? _____
10. Where's John Goode's office? _____
11. Where are the vending machines? _____
    _____
12. Where's Art Jones's office? _____
13. Where's Brian Burns's office? _____
14. Where are the elevators? _____

MAKE IT WORK

Answer the question.

What floor is your classroom on? _____

5

THEY'RE IN THE MEN'S DEPARTMENT.

Possessive of Plural Nouns

Verb *To Be*

plural form	possessive form
boys	boys ['] department
men	men ['s] department

Note: Add an apostrophe (') to form the possessive of plural nouns ending in s. Add 's to form the possessive of plural nouns that do not end in s.

PRACTICE

Answer the questions.

1. Where are T-shirts for men?   *They're in the men's department.*

2. Where are dresses for girls?   _____

3. Where are shoes for men?   _____

4. Where are suits for women?   _____

5. Where are sneakers for boys?   _____

6. Where are shoes for children?   _____

7. Where are nightgowns for girls?   _____

8. Where are dresses for ladies?   _____

9. Where are ties for men?   _____

10. Where are coats for children?   _____

11. Where are socks for boys?   _____

12. Where are blouses for women?   _____

MAKE IT WORK

Fill in the dialogue.

■ Excuse me. Where are clothes for children?

☐ _____

■ Thank you.

IT'S ON THE THIRD FLOOR IN ROOM 307.

Prepositions of Place: *In* and *On*

Verb *To Be*

in	the men's department
in	Room 307
in	the basement
in	aisle seven
in	the main building

basement

on	the third floor
on	the shelf
on	the counter

aisle

PRACTICE

Fill in the dialogues with *in* or *on*.

■ Where are the towels? ☐ They're <u>*in*</u> the bath department.
(1)

■ Where's that? ☐ It's _____ the third floor _____ the main
(2)   (3)

building.

■ Where are your towels? ☐ They're _____ aisle two _____ the shelf.
(4)   (5)

■ Are they on sale? ☐ No. Our sale items are downstairs _____
(6)

the basement.

■ Where's the basement? ☐ The stairs to the basement are _____ the
(7)

first floor.

■ Where are the towels? ☐ They're over there _____ the table.
(8)

■ Are they on sale? ☐ No. The sale items are _____ aisle seven.
(9)

■ Where's the manager's office? ☐ It's _____ the third floor _____ Room 307.
(10)   (11)

■ But I was just _____ the bath department _____ the third floor!
(12)   (13)

7

VALENTINE'S DAY IS ON FEBRUARY 14TH.

Prepositions of Time: *In* and *On*

Verb *To Be*

in	February
on	Saturday
on	February 14th

Note: Use *in* for months.
Use *on* for days.
Use *on* for dates.

PRACTICE

Fill in the blanks about the following American holidays. Use *in* or *on*.

1. Christmas is _on_ December 25th.

2. Thanksgiving is _____ November.

3. Valentine's Day is _____ February 14th.

4. Independence Day is _____ July 4th.

5. Halloween is _____ October.

6. Mother's Day is _____ May.

7. Mother's Day is _____ Sunday.

8. Election Day is _____ the first Tuesday _____ November.

9. Easter is usually _____ April.

10. Father's Day is _____ Sunday.

11. Father's Day is _____ June.

12. St. Patrick's Day is _____ March 17th.

13. New Year's Day is _____ January 1st.

14. Columbus Day is _____ October.

15. New Year's Eve is _____ December 31st.

MAKE IT WORK

Answer the questions.

What's your favorite holiday? _____

When is it? _____

When is your birthday? _____

_____

8

Questions with *What Kind Of, When, Where*
Verb *To Be*

Tony's Restaurant
Great Italian Cooking

Hours: 11:00 – 11:00
Closed holidays

First Floor, Beaman Building
555-5634

What kind of restaurant is Tony's?

It's Italian.

When is it open?

It's open **from** 11:00 **to** 11:00.

When is it closed?

It's closed **on** holidays.

Where is it?

It's **on** the first floor **in** the Beaman Building.

PRACTICE

Make questions with *what kind of, when,* and *where*. Answer your questions.

THANOS'S
COFFEE SHOP

Authentic Food from Greece
Open 6 A.M. – 4:30 P.M.

Located in the Towers Building
Tenth Floor

555-6122
Closed Mondays

Art Wong's Restaurant
Fine Chinese Food

Harbor Boulevard
near Disneyland

Hours: 12:30 – 10:00 P.M.

Closed in August

1. *What kind of restaurant is Thanos's?*
   It's Greek.

2. _____

   _____

3. _____

   _____

4. _____

   _____

5. _____

   _____

6. _____

   _____

7. _____

   _____

8. _____

   _____

Bob's Tacos
Mexican Fast Food

*Open every day except
December 25th*

10:00 A.M. to 12:00 P.M.
Tishman Building, Orange

Pierre's French Restaurant
Fine French Dining

*Dinner Monday–Saturday
6:00 p.m.–9:30 p.m.*

Newport Building
Top Floor
Newport Beach
555-2000

9. _____

10. _____

11. _____

12. _____

13. _____

14. _____

15. _____

16. _____

MAKE IT WORK

Answer the questions.

What's your favorite restaurant? _____

What kind of restaurant is it? _____

When is it open? _____

What day (or days) is it closed? _____

Where is it? _____

New Words: closed = not open   top = highest

WHERE'S ART JONES'S APARTMENT?

Review: Questions with *Where*, Possessives, Ordinal Numbers, Prepositions

Apartment Directory	
3B	Ken Johnson
3A	Connie Rivera
2B	Anita Hug
2A	Art Jones
1B	Samantha Porter
1A	Brian and Carmen Burns
Basement	Superintendent

Where 's Art Jones 's apartment?

It's on the second floor.

contraction: where's = where is

PRACTICE

Look at the apartment directory. Ask questions with *where*. Then answer your questions.

1. Ken Johnson

   Where's Ken Johnson's apartment?

   It's on the third floor.

2. Connie Rivera

   _____

   _____

3. Anita Hug

   _____

   _____

4. Art Jones

   _____

   _____

5. Samantha Porter

   _____

   _____

6. Brian and Carmen Burns

   _____

   _____

7. the superintendent

   _____

   _____

MAKE IT WORK

Fill in the dialogue so that it is correct.

■ Where _'s_ Dr. Chan_____ office?

☐ It's _____ the Chinese Department _____ the six _____ floor.

Negative and Affirmative Statements

There Is and *There Are*

New Words: fire hydrant   street light   parking lot

There's	a bus stop on Green Street.
There isn't	a park on Green Street.
There are	sidewalks on Green Street.
There aren't	(any) street lights on Green Street.

contractions: isn't = is not   aren't = are not   there's = there is

Note: Do not contract *there are*.

PRACTICE

Look at the picture on page 12. Then tell about Green Street. Use negative or affirmative sentences with *there is* and *there are*.

1. three houses   *There are three houses on Green Street.*

2. a laundromat   _____

3. a bus stop   _____

4. trees   _____

5. an apartment building   _____

6. street lights   _____

7. a drugstore   _____

8. a gas station   _____

9. two mailboxes   _____

10. sidewalks   _____

11. a fire hydrant   _____

12. a grocery store   _____

13. a parking lot   _____

14. a park   _____

MAKE IT WORK

Tell about your street.

There _____

_____

_____

_____

13

ARE THERE HOUSES ON GREEN STREET?

Yes-No Questions

There Is and *There Are*

> There are apartments on Green Street.
>
> Are there   houses   on Green Street?

 PRACTICE

Fill in the blanks with *Is there* or *Are there*.

1. *Are there*   office buildings on Green Street?
2. _____ trees on Green Street?
3. _____ a fire hydrant on Green Street?
4. _____ apartments on Green Street?
5. _____ a park?
6. _____ sidewalks?
7. _____ a parking lot?
8. _____ street lights?
9. _____ a bus stop?
10. _____ stores?
11. _____ a gas station?
12. _____ mailboxes?
13. _____ a newsstand?
14. _____ a laundromat?

MAKE IT WORK

Ask two important questions about Green Street.

> House for Sale
> 28 Green Street
> 555-5967

Are there street lights on Green Street? _____

_____

_____

THERE'S SOME RICE IN THE CABINET.

Some with Countable and Uncountable Nouns

There Is and *There Are*

There are | some | potatoes in the cabinet.
There's | some | rice in the cabinet.

Note: Use *some* in affirmative statements with uncountable nouns and with plural countable nouns. Use singular verb forms with uncountable nouns.

salt	pepper	flour	tea
oil	coffee	sugar	rice

PRACTICE

Look at the picture above. Then tell what's in the cabinet.

1. *There's some salt in the cabinet.*

2. _____

3. _____

4. _____

5. _____

6. _____

7. _____

8. _____

9. _____

10. _____

11. _____

12. _____

THERE AREN'T ANY LEFT.

Any with Countable and Uncountable Nouns

There Is and There Are

> There are some carrots left.
>
> There aren't any carrots left.   There aren't any left.
>
> Note: Use *any* in negative statements with uncountable nouns and with plural countable nouns. Use singular verb forms with uncountable nouns.
>
> meat   salad   rice
>
> bread   mustard

PRACTICE

Make negative sentences with *any*.

1. Please pass the carrots.   *There aren't any left.*
2. Please pass the rice.   _____
3. Please pass the peas.   _____
4. Please pass the potatoes.   _____
5. Pass the salad, please.   _____
6. Please pass the meat.   _____
7. Pass the tomatoes, please.   _____
8. Pass the mustard, please.   _____
9. Pass the bread, please.   _____
10. Please pass the eggs.   _____

MAKE IT WORK

Fill in the dialogue.

■ Please pass the meat.

☐ I'm sorry. There _____

■ Then can you pass the potatoes?

☐ There _____ potatoes, either.

New Words: left = remaining, not eaten

salad = kind of food usually made with lettuce

THERE ARE SOME KEYS IN GLORIA'S PURSE.

Some and *Any* with Countable and Uncountable Nouns

There Is and *There Are*

There are ~~some~~ keys in Gloria's purse.

There aren't ~~any~~ sunglasses in Gloria's purse.

Note: uncountable nouns:

money medicine makeup gum candy

PRACTICE

What's in Gloria's purse? Look at the picture above. Then make negative or affirmative sentences. Use contractions whenever possible.

1. (money)   *There's some money in Gloria's purse.*

2. (pens) _____

3. (makeup) _____

4. (tissues) _____

5. (medicine) _____

6. (gum) _____

7. (sunglasses) _____

8. (credit cards) _____

9. (keys) _____

10. (combs) _____

11. (candy) _____

12. (business cards) _____

MAKE IT WORK

Tell what's in your wallet.

_____

_____

_____

_____

HOW MUCH MILK IS THERE?

Questions with *How Much* and *How Many*

There Is* and *There Are

> There's some milk in the refrigerator.
> How much milk is there?
>
> There are some carrots in the refrigerator.
> How many carrots are there?
>
> Note: Use *how many* with countable nouns. Use *how much* with uncountable nouns.
>
> milk   cheese   lettuce   soda   chicken
> steak   oil   juice   bread

PRACTICE

Make questions with *how much* or *how many.*

1. There's some milk in the refrigerator.   *How much milk is there?*

2. There's some cheese in the refrigerator.   _____

3. There are some eggs in the refrigerator.   _____

4. There's some orange juice in the
   refrigerator.   _____

5. There are some apples in the basket.   _____

6. There's some steak in the refrigerator.   _____

7. There are some strawberries in the
   refrigerator.   _____

8. There are some potatoes in the cabinet.   _____

9. There's some lettuce in the refrigerator.   _____

10. There are some cookies in the cabinet.   _____

11. There's some oil in the refrigerator.   _____

12. There's some chicken in the refrigerator. _____

13. There are some tomatoes in the
    refrigerator.   _____

14. There's some bread in the refrigerator.   _____

ALL RIGHT, BUT JUST A LITTLE, PLEASE.

A Little and A Few

> How about some more coffee?
> All right, but just a little, please.
>
> How about some more cookies?
> All right, but just a few.
>
> Note: *a little* and *a few* = a small quantity
> Use *a few* with countable nouns; use *a little* with uncountable nouns.

PRACTICE

Answer the questions with *a little* or *a few*.

1. How about some more meat? *All right, but just a little.*
2. How about some more milk? _____
3. How about some more potato chips? _____
4. How about some more salad? _____
5. How about some more carrots? _____
6. How about some more bread? _____
7. How about some more crackers? _____
8. How about some more cheese? _____
9. How about some more soda? _____
10. How about some more pretzels? _____
11. How about some more chicken? _____
12. How about some more strawberries? _____
13. How about some more hot coffee? _____
14. How about some more tomatoes? _____

MAKE IT WORK

Answer the question.

■ How about some mustard on your sandwich?

☐ _____

Partitives

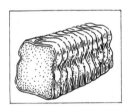

a [box of]
strawberries
crackers
cookies
cereal

a [bottle of]
soda
oil
salad dressing

a [can of]
soup
tunafish
peas

a [bag of]
potato chips
pretzels

a [jar of]
mayonnaise
mustard

a [loaf of] bread

a [head of] lettuce

a [quart of]
milk
juice

a [pound of]
potatoes
butter
tomatoes
meat
chicken

a [dozen]
eggs
rolls

Equivalents: one pound = .45 kilogram
one quart = .95 liter

2 LOAVES OF BREAD

1	can of soup	2	boxes of crackers
1	dozen rolls	2	loaves of bread

Note: Partitives are used to express quantity. They can be used before countable and uncountable nouns.

irregular plural: loaf → loaves

PRACTICE

Fill in the grocery list.

1. 2 _____boxes of_____ crackers
2. 2 _____ soda
3. 2 _____ tunafish
4. 2 _____ potato chips
5. 1 _____ mayonnaise
6. 2 _____ milk
7. 2 _____ bread
8. 5 _____ potatoes
9. 2 _____ lettuce
10. 2 _____ wine
11. 4 _____ chicken
12. 1 _____ eggs
13. 1 _____ salad dressing
14. 1 _____ mustard
15. 3 _____ tomato soup

MAKE IT WORK

Make a list of some things you need from the supermarket.

_____   _____

_____   _____

_____   _____

_____   _____

_____   _____

TWO SLICES OF PIZZA, PLEASE.

Partitives

a | glass of | milk juice soda   a | cup of | tea coffee   a | piece of | candy cake pie

a | bowl of | soup cereal   a | dish of | ice cream   a | slice of | pizza bread

Note: An uncountable noun can be counted when a partitive is used before it: orange juice → two glasses of orange juice.

PRACTICE

Make plural sentences. Begin with the word *two*.

1. Some orange juice, please.   _Two glasses of orange juice, please._

2. Some coffee, please.   _____

3. Some soda, please.   _____

4. Some chocolate cake, please.   _____

5. Some vegetable soup, please.   _____

6. Some water, please.   _____

7. Some vanilla ice cream, please.   _____

8. Some apple pie, please.   _____

9. Some milk, please.   _____

10. Some pizza, please.   _____

11. Some cereal, please.   _____

12. Some tea, please.   _____

MAKE IT WORK

Look at the dialogue. Then write what both customers ordered.

Waitress: Can I take your order?
Customer 1: Yes. I'd like a hamburger, apple pie, and coffee.
Customer 2: Some vegetable soup, a hamburger, apple pie, and coffee, please.

_____

_____

_____

2 POUNDS OF HAMBURGER MEAT.

Review: Countable and Uncountable Nouns, Partitives

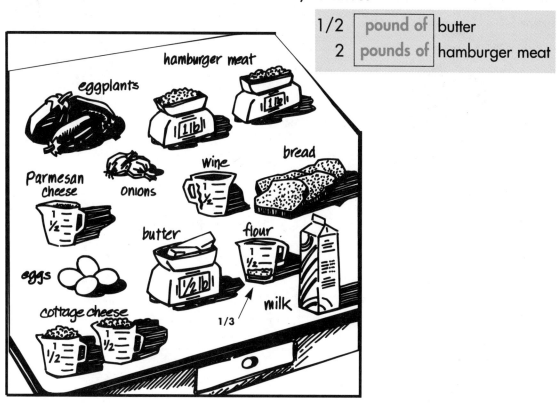

1/2	pound of	butter
2	pounds of	hamburger meat

PRACTICE

Moussaka is a Greek dish. Look at the picture and tell what's in it.

1. _3 eggplants_
2. _____
3. _____
4. _____
5. _____
6. _____

7. _____
8. _____
9. _____
10. _____
11. _____

MAKE IT WORK

Answer the questions.

What's your favorite dish? _____

What's in it? _____ _____

_____ _____

_____ _____

_____ _____

THERE ISN'T ANYTHING IN MY HAND.

Something **and** *Anything*

There Is

There's something in my hand.

There isn't anything in my hand.

Note: Use *something* and *anything* for unspecified things. Use *something* in affirmative statements. Use *anything* in negative statements.

PRACTICE

Look at the pictures. Then make sentences with *something* or *anything*.

1. *There isn't anything* _____ in the hat.

2. Now _____ in the hat.

3. _____ in my hand.

4. Now _____ in my hand.

5. _____ under the scarf.

6. Now _____ under the scarf.

7. _____ up my sleeve.

8. Now _____ up my sleeve.

9. _____ in my pocket.

10. Now _____ in my pocket.

THERE'S NO ONE BEHIND THE CURTAIN.

Someone and *No One*

There Is

There's [someone] behind the curtain.

There's [no one] behind the curtain.

Note: Use *someone* and *no one* for unspecified people. *No one* expresses a negative idea. Do not use *no one* with negative verbs.

PRACTICE

Look at the pictures. Then make sentences with *someone* or *no one*.

1.  *There's someone* _____ under the scarf.

2.  Now _____ under the scarf.

3. _____ behind the curtain.

4. Now _____ behind the curtain.

5.  _____ in the chair.

6. Now _____ in the chair.

7.  _____ in the box.

8.  Now _____ in the box.

HE'S TAKING A SHOWER NOW.

Affirmative Statements
Present Continuous

He | 's cooking | now.
They | 're studying | now.

study → ing = studying   take → ing = taking   cook → ing = cooking

Note: To form the present continuous, add *ing* to the verb. If a verb ends in *y*, add *ing*. If a verb ends in *e*, omit the *e* and add *ing*.

PRACTICE
Answer the questions.

1. Is Brian there? (cook)   _Yes, but he's cooking now._

2. Is Linda there? (sleep)   _____

3. Is John there? (take a shower) _____

4. Is Barbara there? (wash her hair) _____

5. Are your parents there? (eat dinner) _____

6. Is your mother there?   _____
   (watch the baby)   _____

7. Is Andy there? (study)   _____

8. Are Bruce and Susan at there?   _____
   (work in the yard)   _____

9. Is Diane there? (iron)   _____

10. Is Susan there? (water the plants) _____

11. Is Carmen there? (practice the piano) _____

12. Are Dorothy and Leonard there? _____
    (wash the car)   _____

MAKE IT WORK

Fill in the dialogue.

■ Hello.

 Hi. This is _____. Is _____ there?

■ Yes, but _____. May I take a message?

□ No, thanks. I'll call back later.

26

THE PEOPLE ARE SITTING IN THEIR SEATS.

Spelling

Present Continuous

one-syllable

clap → clap [ping]

shut → shut [ting]

Note: For one-syllable verbs ending in a single vowel + a consonant, double the consonant before adding *ing*.

clap → clapping
└─ vowel
  └─ consonant

two-syllable

begín → begin [ning]

admít → admit [ting]

For two-syllable verbs with stress on the second syllable, double the last consonant before adding *ing*.

admít   consonant → admitting
      └─ vowel
        └─ consonant

Note: Don't double the final consonant for two-syllable verbs with stress on the first syllable: ópen → ópening.

Don't double w, x, or y.

PRACTICE

Add *ing* to the verbs below. Be sure to double the consonant or cross out the *e* ($\cancel{e}$) if necessary

1. The people are sit_ting_ in their seats.

2. The show is begín_____.

3. The curtain is go_____ up.

4. Some people are clap____.

5. Some people are still talk_____.

6. Some people are whísper_____

7. Some people are smile_____

8. Some people are ópen_____ their programs.

9. Some people are read_____ their programs.

10. Some people are take_____ off their coats.

11. Some people are lísten_____ to the music.

12. Some people are look_____ at the stage.

13. Some people are point_____ at the stage.

14. Some people are put_____ on their glasses.

15. Some people are wear_____ blue jeans.

New Word: clapping

27

THE MAN IS SITTING NEXT TO A YOUNG WOMAN.

Prepositions of Place: *In, Next To, Between, Behind, In Front Of*

Present Continuous

| next to | between | behind | in front of |

PRACTICE

Look at the picture below. Then fill in the blanks with *in, next to, between, behind,* or *in front of.*

1. The people are sitting _*in*_____ a movie theater.

2. They're sitting _____ their seats.

3. A man is sitting _____ the front row.

4. The man is sitting _____ a young woman.

5. The man is also sitting _____ an elderly woman.

6. The man is sitting _____ the young woman and the elderly woman.

7. The elderly woman is wearing a large hat. She's sitting _____ a boy.

8. The boy is sitting _____ the elderly woman. He's frowning.

New Word: elderly = old

28

THEY'RE LOOKING AT HIM.

Subject and Object Pronouns

Present Continuous

I	'm	looking at	you,	and	you're	looking at	me.
You	're	looking at	us,	and	we're	looking at	you.
He	's	looking at	them,	and	they're	looking at	him.
She	's	looking at	me,	and	I'm	looking at	her.
We	're	looking at	her,	and	she's	looking at	us.
They	're	looking at	him,	and	he's	looking at	them.

PRACTICE

Complete the sentences with the present continuous and the correct pronouns.

1. They're looking at him, and _he's looking at them._ _____

2. I'm looking at you, and _____

3. He's looking at us, and _____

4. They're looking at her, and _____

5. We're watching them, and _____

6. She's watching you, and _____

7. He's watching me, and _____

8. You're talking to us, and _____

9. I'm talking to him, and _____

10. They're talking to her, and _____

11. We're listening to them, and _____

12. She's listening to me, and _____

MAKE IT WORK

Look at the picture. Then fill in the blanks with the correct pronouns

The tall man is talking to the short woman, but she isn't listening to _him_____. She's looking at the man in the corner. The man in the corner is looking at _____. He's smiling at_____, and she's smiling at _____.

29

THE CAT IS RUNNING TOWARD THE TREE.

Prepositions of Place and Direction

Present Continuous

The cat is sitting	in	the cage.
The cat is sitting	on	the cage.
The cat is sitting	near	the cage.

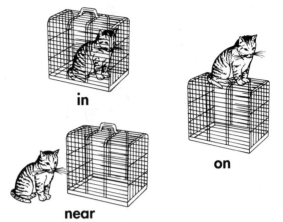

in

on

near

under

away from

The cat is sitting	under	the tree.
The cat is running	away from	the tree.
The cat is running	toward(s)	the tree.
The cat is running	up	the tree.

toward

up

The cat is running	down	the tree.
The cat is running	around	the tree.

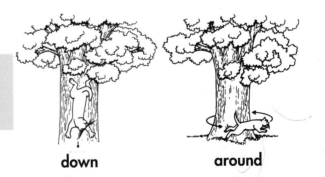

down

around

PRACTICE

Look at the pictures below. Then make sentences with the present continuous and one of the prepositions above.

1.   (sit) The cat _is sitting in the cage._ _____

       _____

2.   (sit) The bird _____

       _____

3.   (run) The cat _____

       _____

4.   (sit) The cat _____

       _____

5.   (run) The cat _____

       _____

6.   (fly) The bird _____

       _____

7.   (run) The cat _____

       _____

8.   (run) The cat _____

       _____

9.   (sit) The bird _____

       _____

10.   (run) The cat _____

       _____

11.   (fly) The bird _____

       _____

12.   (sit) The cat _____

       _____

THE PRESIDENT IS WAVING AND SMILING.

Combining Sentences with *And*

Present Continuous

	verb
The president	is waving.
The president	is smiling.
The president	is waving and smiling.

Note: You can combine two sentences with the same subject and different verbs. Drop the second *is* when the two sentences are combined.

	subject	
The president		is shaking hands.
The king		is shaking hands.
The president and	the king	are shaking hands.

Note: You can combine two sentences with the same verb and different subjects. Notice that *is* changes to *are* when two subjects are combined.

subject	**verb**
The president	is smiling.
The king	is talking.
The president is smiling , and	the king is talking.

Note: You can combine two different sentences. Put a comma (,) before *and* when two entire sentences are combined.

PRACTICE

Combine the sentences.

1. This is Channel 30 News.

   I'm Connie Rivera at the airport in London.

   This is Channel 30 News, and I'm Connie Rivera at the airport in London.

2. The president is getting out of the plane now.

   The first lady is getting out of the plane now.

   _____

3. The president is smiling at the people.

   The president is waving at the people.

   _____

4. Now the president is walking down the stairs.

    Now the first lady is walking down the stairs.

    _____

    _____

5. The president is shaking hands.

    The king is shaking hands.

    _____

    _____

6. The first lady is talking to the queen.

    The queen is smiling.

    _____

    _____

7. The queen is wearing a suit.

    The first lady is wearing a dress.

    _____

    _____

8. The king is getting into a limousine.

    The president is getting into a limousine.

    _____

    _____

9. The first lady is getting into a limousine.

    The queen is getting into a limousine.

    _____

    _____

10. The people are waving.

    The people are shouting.

    _____

    _____

New Word: limousine

HE ISN'T LOOKING AT THE CAMERA.

Negative and Affirmative Statements

Present Continuous

| The groom | isn't looking | at the camera. |
| The bride and groom | aren't looking | at the camera. |

P R A C T I C E

Look at the picture above. Then fill in the blanks with negative or affirmative verbs. Use contractions whenever possible.

1. (take)   The photographer _is taking_ a picture of the bride and groom.

2. (stand)   The photographer _____ up.

3. (stand)   The bride and groom _____ up.

4. (look)   They _____ at the camera.

5. (look)   They _____ at the cake.

6. (hold)   They _____ glasses of champagne.

7. (hold)   They _____ a knife.

8. (kiss)   They _____.

9. (cut)   They _____ the cake.

10. (wear)   The bride _____ an evening dress.

11. (wear)   She _____ a wedding dress.

12. (wear)   The groom _____ a tuxedo.

13. (smile)   She _____.

14. (smile)   He _____.

New Words: champagne   tuxedo   bride   groom

WHAT ARE YOU LAUGHING AT?

Questions with *Who* and *What*

Present Continuous

> She's laughing at someone.   I'm laughing at something.
> **Who**'s she laughing at?   **What** are you laughing at?
>
> Note: Use *who* questions for someone (a person);
>   use *what* questions for something (a thing).
>
>   contractions: who's = who is   what's = what is

PRACTICE

Make questions with *who* or *what*. Use contractions whenever possible.

1. I'm smiling at something. (you)   *What are you smiling at?*

2. He's frowning at something.   _____

3. They're laughing at something.   _____

4. She's yelling at someone.   _____

5. I'm smiling at someone. (you)   _____

6. They're listening to someone.   _____

7. He's waving at someone.   _____

8. I'm looking at something. (you)   _____

9. We're laughing at someone. (you)   _____

10. They're clapping at something.   _____

11. She's talking to someone.   _____

12. He's listening to something.   _____

MAKE IT WORK

Ask two questions about the woman in the picture.

What's she talking about?   _____

_____

_____

THEY'RE WAITING IN LINE.

Review: Present Continuous

A boy is in a telephone booth.

A man | is waiting | in line.

Four people | are waiting | in line.

P R A C T I C E

Look at the picture above. Then make some sentences about what is happening in the picture. Use contractions whenever possible.

1. A young boy *is talking*_____ on the telephone.

2. He _____ to his mother.

3. Four people _____ in line.

4. They _____ to use the telephone.

5. A man _____ the newspaper.

6. A teenage girl _____ at the boy in the telephone booth.

7. An elderly woman in a wheelchair _____ at her watch.

8. The woman behind her _____ a baby.

9. The baby _____ .

10. The people in line _____

_____

CHANG IS GOING TO WATCH THE FIREWORKS IN THE PARK.

Affirmative Statements

Future with *Going To*

I	'm going to go	to a party on the Fourth of July.
Chang	is going to watch	the fireworks in the park.
Gloria and Oscar	are going to have	a picnic in the park.

Note: Use *going to* for a future event when you are fairly certain the event will occur.

PRACTICE

Fill in the blanks with the correct form of the future with *going to*.

1. (watch) Chang *is going to watch* the fireworks in the park.

2. (go) Akira _____ to the street fair.

3. (watch) Rosa and her husband _____ the fireworks on TV.

4. (stay) Loi _____ at home.

5. (have) Gloria and Oscar _____ a picnic in the park.

6. (go) Florie and Bob _____ to a party.

7. (take) Rafael _____ a drive.

8. (go) John and Marie _____ to a parade.

9. (have) Mohsen and his friends _____ a barbecue.

10. (visit) Julia _____ relatives.

11. (work) Louise and Raymond _____ in the yard.

12. (go) Anna _____ shopping.

MAKE IT WORK

Answer the questions.

When is your next holiday? _____

What are you going to do? _____

_____

_____

_____

WE'RE HUNGRY, SO WE'RE GOING TO EAT.

Combining Sentences with *So*

Future with *Going To*

> We're hungry. We're going to eat.
> We're hungry $\boxed{, so}$ we're going to eat.
>
> Note: Use *so* for result. When combining two sentences with *so*, put a comma between the two sentences.

 PRACTICE

Complete the sentences with *so* and *going to*. Use the choices below.

go to bed	✔ take some aspirin
go to the dentist	put on a sweater
watch television	drink some water
visit some friends	get some help
see a doctor	ask for directions

1. I have a headache, *so I'm going to take some aspirin.*
2. She's thirsty _____
3. He has a toothache _____
4. I'm lonely _____
5. He's tired _____
6. She's cold _____
7. They're in trouble _____
8. I'm sick _____
9. She's lost _____
10. We're bored _____

MAKE IT WORK

Make a statement about yourself. Then tell what you're going to do.

I'm bored, so I'm going to read a book.

_____

_____

THEY AREN'T GOING TO HAVE A BIG WEDDING.

Negative Statements

Furture with *Going To*

Jennifer and Eric	are	going to have	a big wedding.
Sonia and Peter	aren't	going to have	a big wedding.
Sonia	isn't	going to wear	a wedding dress.

PRACTICE

Read about Jennifer and Eric's wedding. Then make the sentences negative. Tell about Sonia and Peter. Change *Jennifer* to *Sonia* and *Eric* to *Peter*. Use contractions whenever possible.

Jennifer and Eric are going to have a big wedding. They're going to be married in a big church. They're going to invite a lot of people to their wedding. Jennifer is going to wear a wedding dress. She's going to carry flowers. Eric is going to wear a tuxedo. Jennifer and Eric are going to have a big reception after the wedding. They're going to have a cake, and they're going to serve champagne. They're going to have a band. Afterward they're going to go on a honeymoon.

Sonia and Peter aren't going to have a big wedding.

_____

_____

_____

_____

_____

_____

_____

_____

_____

_____

_____

_____

New Words: reception = a party after a wedding

honeymoon = a trip a newly married couple takes

WHEN IS THE PARTY GOING TO BE?

Questions with *When, What, Where, Whose*
Future with *Going To*

Date:	July 4th
Time:	5:00–9:00
Place:	Marie DuLac's
	17620 LaCuarta Street
	Los Angeles
	(213) 555-1120

Bring your favorite drink.
Dress casually.

The party isn't going to be on July 3rd.
When is it going to be?

PRACTICE

Look at the invitation. Make questions with *when, what,* or *where.*

1. The party isn't going to be on July 3rd.   When *is it going to be?*

2. The party isn't going to be a Halloween party.   What kind _____

   _____

3. The party isn't going to start at 4:00.   What time _____

4. The party isn't going to end at 12:00.   What time _____

5. The party isn't going to be at Julia Santos's house.   Where _____

   _____

6. The party isn't going to be at 17600 La Cuarta Street.   Where _____

   _____

7. The party isn't going to be in June.   When _____

8. The guests aren't going to bring dessert.   What _____

9. The guests aren't going to wear fancy clothes.   What _____

   _____

10. Marie's telephone number isn't 555-1100.   What _____

   _____

MAYBE THEY'LL GET MARRIED NEXT YEAR.

Affirmative Statements

Future with *Will*

> Chang | will take | another English class.
> He | 'll take | ESL 3.
>
> Note: Use *will* for future events. Use *will* when you are less certain an event will occur.
>
>   (more certain) They're going to get married tomorrow.
>   (less certain)   Maybe they'll get married next year.
>
> contractions: he'll = he will   she'll = she will   they'll = they will

PRACTICE

What will the students in ESL 2 do when the course is over? Fill in the blanks with the correct form of the future with *will*. Use contractions with pronouns.

1. (take)   Chang _will take_____ another English class.

   (take)   He _'ll take_____ ESL 3.

2. (go)   Rosa _____ back to school in the fall.

   (study)   She _____ nursing.

3. (travel)   Gloria and Oscar _____ .

   (visit)   They _____ their families in Spain.

4. (look)   Loi _____ for a better job.

5. (take)   Rafael and his wife _____ a class in pronunciation at the community college.

6. (get married) Maybe John and Marie _____ .

7. (get)   Mohsen _____ a job.

8. (work)   Anna _____ in her parents' restaurant.

   (study)   Also, she _____ accounting at the university.

9. (return)   Akira _____ to his country.

   (work)   He _____ for his father in Tokyo.

10. (ask)   Because Carlo's English is better, he _____ his boss for a promotion!

YOU WILL LIVE A LONG LIFE.

Affirmative Statements: Predictions

Future with *Will*

You		
Your husband	will live	a long life.
You and your husband		
Your children		

Note: Use *will* for future events. *Will* is sometimes used for predictions about the future.

PRACTICE

Fill in the blanks with *will* and the verb in parentheses.

1. (go)   You _will go_____ on a long trip.

2. (meet) You _____ a stranger.

3. (be)   He _____ tall, dark, and handsome.

4. (fall)   You _____ in love.

5. (marry) You _____ him.

6. (have)   You and your husband _____ a lot of money.

7. (be)   Your husband _____ a successful architect.

8. (have)   You _____ six children.

9. (move) You and your family _____ to a foreign country.

10. (live)   You _____ in a beautiful house.

11. (be)   One of your children _____ famous.

12. (get)   Al of your children _____ married.

13. have)   You _____ a lot of grandchildren.

14. (live)   You _____ a long life.

15. (be)   You _____ very happy.

MAKE IT WORK

Make two predictions about your future.

_____ _I will_ _____

_____

WILL I RETURN TO MY COUNTRY?

Yes-No Questions: Predictions

Future with *Will*

Will I   return to my country?
You will return to your country.

PRACTICE

Look at the chart below. Then ask some questions about the future.

Will	I my husband (or wife) my children	get change go win be live have	the lottery? jobs? to college? rich? a long life? famous? a lot of children? married? divorced? happy? a lot of money? successful? healthy?

1. *Will my husband change jobs?*
2. _____
3. _____
4. _____
5. _____
6. _____
7. _____
8. _____
9. _____
10. _____
11. _____
12. _____

WILL FLORIE TAKE ANOTHER ENGLISH CLASS? NO, SHE WON'T.

Negative and Affirmative Short Answers

Future with *Will*

I probably won't take another English class. I'll travel to the Philippines this summer. My husband will be sixty next year, and he'll retire. We'll move to Las Vegas and buy a house there.

Will Florie take another English class?
Will she travel to the Philippines?

contraction: won't = will not

No she won't.
Yes, she will.

PRACTICE

Read about Florie's plans. Then answer the questions with short answers.

1. Will Florie get a job? _No, she won't._

2. Will she take another English class? _____

3. Will she study at the university? _____

4. Will her husband be sixty next year? _____

5. Will he work next year? _____

6. Will he retire? _____

7. Will Florie travel this summer? _____

8. Will she travel around the United States? _____

9. Will Florie and her husband move
   to the Philippines? _____

10. Will they move to Las Vegas? _____

11. Will they buy a house in the Philippines? _____

12. Will they buy a house in Las Vegas? _____

MAKE IT WORK

Answer the question with a short answer.

Will you take another English class next semester? _____

THEY WON'T HELP AROUND THE HOUSE.

Negative Statements: Refusal

Future with *Will*

They won't help around the house.

Note: Use *won't* to express refusal.

PRACTICE

John and Barbara Burns live at home. They refuse to do anything their parents tell them. Make sentences with *won't*. Begin your sentences with a pronoun.

1. John refuses to clean his room.   *He won't clean his room.*

2. Barbara refuses to hang up her clothes. _____

   _____

3. John and Barbara refuse to make _____

   their beds. _____

4. John refuses to take out the trash. _____

5. John and Barbara refuse to eat vegetables. _____

   _____

6. Barbara refuses to wash the dishes. _____

7. John refuses to walk the dog. _____

8. Barbara refuses to feed the dog. _____

9. John refuses to get a part-time job. _____

10. John and Barbara refuse to help _____

    around the house. _____

11. Barbara refuses to practice the piano. _____

    _____

12. John refuses to mow the lawn. _____

MAKE IT WORK

Name two chores you won't do.

I won't _____

_____

New Word: part-time job = a job that is fewer than 40 hours a week

45

I WON'T RETURN TO MY COUNTRY THIS YEAR.

Review: Future with _Will_

| I | 'll return | to my country this year. |
| I | won't return | to my country this year. |

contraction: I'll = I will

PRACTICE

Tell which things you'll do this year and which things you won't do this year.
Use contractions whenever possible.

1. take a vacation   _I'll take a vacation this year._

           or   _I won't take a vacation this year._

2. get married   _____

3. move   _____

4. return to my country   _____

    _____

5. become a U. S. citizen   _____

    _____

6. take another English class   _____

    _____

7. study at the university   _____

    _____

8. get a new job   _____

9. finish GrammarWork 2   _____

10. retire   _____

11. get a promotion at work   _____

    _____

12. learn another language   _____

MAKE IT WORK

Name the most important thing you'll do or won't do next year.

_____

I'LL BE A FAMOUS ARTIST IN TEN YEARS.

Contrast: Future with *Will,* Present Continuous, Verb *To Be*

I | ' m studying | art now.

I | ' ll be | a famous artist in ten years.

PRACTICE

Answer the questions.

1. What class (or classes) are you taking now?
   I'm taking English.

2. What school are you studying at?

3. What book (or books) are you using?

4. What will you do when this course is over?

5. What's your present occupation?

6. What will you be ten years from now? What job will you have?

7. How old are you?

8. How old will you be on your next birthday?

9. What's the weather like today?

10. What will the weather probably be like tomorrow?

11. What country are you from?

12. What country are you living in now?

HE COLLECTS SHELLS.

Affirmative Statements

Simple Present

My hobby is collecting shells.	I	collect shells.
Your hobby is collecting shells.	You	collect shells.
His hobby is collecting shells.	He	collects shells.
Her hobby is collecting shells.	She	collects shells.
Our hobby is collecting shells.	We	collect shells.
Their hobby is collecting shells.	They	collect shells.

PRACTICE

Make sentences with collect or collects.

1. His hobby is collecting shells. _He collects shells._____

2. My hobby is collecting stamps. _____

3. Our hobby is collecting coins. _____

4. Her hobby is collecting dolls. _____

5. Their hobby is collecting buttons. _____

6. His hobby is collecting baseball cards. _____

7. My hobby is collecting antiques. _____

8. Her hobby is collecting collecting
   matchbooks. _____

9. His hobby is collecting postcards. _____

10. Their hobby is collecting old records. _____

MAKE IT WORK

Answer the questions.

What's your hobby? _____

What do you collect? _____

New Words: hobby = something people like to do in their free time
            antique = something made more than 100 years ago

doll    button

48

YOLANDA DOESN'T TAKE THE TRAIN.

Negative Statements

Simple Present

Art		takes	the train.
Yolanda	doesn't	take	the train.
I	don't	take	the train.

contractions: doesn't = does not   don't = do not

PRACTICE

Read about Art's commute. Then make the sentences negative. Tell about Yolanda. Change *he* to *she* and *his* to *her*.

1. Art lives in New Jersey.   *Yolanda doesn't live in New Jersey.*

2. He commutes three hours   *She* _____
    a day.   _____

3. He takes the train.   _____

4. He gets up at 5:30.   _____

5. He drives to the train station. _____
    _____

6. He waits for the train.   _____

7. He arrives in New York at 8:00. _____
    _____

8. He takes a bus to his office.   _____

9. Then he walks to his office.   _____

10. He arrives at his office late.   _____

MAKE IT WORK

Fill in the blanks. You can make negative or affirmative sentences.

I _____ to work. I _____ the bus to work.
    (walk)   (take)

I _____ to work. I _____ the train to work.
    (drive)   (take)

49

THEY DON'T GET UP EARLY.

Negative Statements

Simple Present

I		up early.	He		up early.
They	don't get		She	doesn't get	

PRACTICE

Make negative sentences about Gloria and Oscar.

On weekdays: **On the weekend:**

1. Gloria and Oscar work hard.   *Gloria and Oscar don't work hard.*

2. They get up early.   _____

3. They have a quick breakfast.   _____

4. Gloria takes the bus to work. Gloria _____

5. She arrives at work at 9:00.   _____

6. She decorates people's houses _____
   all day.   _____

7. Oscar drives to work.   Oscar _____

8. He works from 8:00 to 5:00.   _____

9. He works in a dentist's office. _____

10. He sees patients all day.   _____

11. He gets home at 6:00.   _____

12. He fixes dinner.   _____

13. Gloria gets home at 7:00.   Gloria _____

14. They go to bed early.   _____

MAKE IT WORK

Name two things you do during   Name two things you don't do on the
the week.   weekend.

I commute to work.   *I don't commute to work.*

_____   _____

_____   _____

50

I LIKE SPORTS PROGRAMS.

Like + Noun

Simple Present

I like sports programs.   I don't like comedies.

PRACTICE

What kind of television programs do you like? Make sentences with *I like* or *I don't like*.

1. comedies   _I like comedies._ _____

2. cartoons   _____

3. dramas   _____

4. old movies   _____

5. talk shows   _____

6. variety shows   _____

7. game shows   _____

8. sports programs   _____

9. the news   _____

10. commercials   _____

MAKE IT WORK

Answer the questions.

What's your favorite television program? _____

What kind of program is it? _____

I LIKE TO WATCH TV.

Like + Infinitive

Simple Present

I	like to watch	TV.
I	don't like to read.	

Note: *Like* can be followed by an infinitive (*to* + simple form of the verb.)

PRACTICE

Look at the chart below. Then make some sentences about yourself.

I	like don't like	to watch to go to to wash to read to listen to to clean to cook to get up to iron	the movies. the house. the radio. the dishes. parties. early. late. concerts. baseball games. television.

1. *I like to watch baseball games.* _____

2. _____

3. _____

4. _____

5. _____

6. _____

7. _____

8. _____

9. _____

10. _____

11. _____

12. _____

SHE LIKES BOOKS. SHE LIKES TO READ.

Like + Noun and Like + Infinitive

Simple Present

> She | likes to read. |
>
> She | likes | good books.
>
> Note: *Like* can be followed by a noun or a verb.
> When it is followed by a verb, use the infinitive form.

PRACTICE

Fill in the blanks with *like(s)* or *like(s) to*.

1. They *like to* _____ watch television.
2. They _____ talk shows.
3. I _____ cowboy movies.
4. I _____ go to the movies.
5. He _____ listen to music.
6. He _____ country music.
7. We _____ tennis.
8. We _____ play tennis.
9. He _____ soccer.
10. He _____ watch soccer games.
11. I _____ good food.
12. I _____ cook.
13. She _____ music.
14. She _____ go to rock concerts.
15. We _____ eat out.
16. We _____ Mexican food.

MAKE IT WORK

Name two things you like.

I like Italian food.

_____

_____

Name two things you like to do.

I like to cook.

_____

_____

53

I NEED TO TAKE SOME LESSONS.

Verb + Noun and Verb + Infinitive

Simple Present

I	like	golf.	I	like to play	golf.
I	need	some lessons.	I	need to take	some lessons.
I	want	some new golf clubs.	I	want to buy	some new golf clubs.

Note: When *want* and *need* are followed by a verb, use the infinitive form.

PRACTICE

Fill in the blanks with *like* or *like to, need* or *need to, want* or *want to.*

John Burns

I <u>*like*</u> country music. I _____
(1. like)   (2. like)

play the guitar, and I'm a pretty good singer.

Someday I _____ be the next Garth
(3. want)

Brooks, but first I _____ a new guitar.
(4. need)

I _____ work in my garden. I _____
(5. like)   (6. like)

flowers, and I _____ be outdoors. This
(7. like)

year I _____ plant a vegetable garden. I
(8. want)

_____ fresh vegetables. The vegetables at
(9. like)

the supermarket just aren't very fresh.

Susan Burns

Brian Burns

I _____ golf, and I play golf every
(10. like)

weekend. I _____ become a good golfer,
(11. want)

but I _____ take some golf lessons. I
(12. need)

_____ watch golf games on TV. I learn a
(13. like)

lot when I watch people play.

I LIKE THE STRIPED ONES.

Pronouns *One* and *Ones*

Simple Present

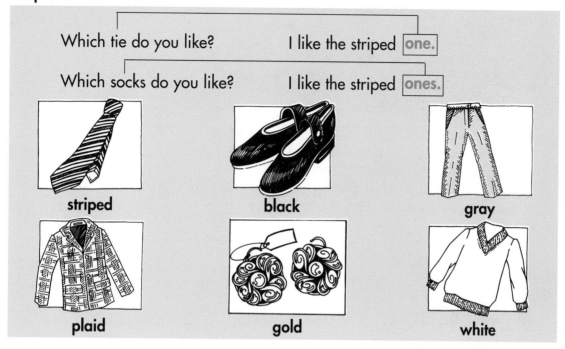

Which tie do you like?   I like the striped one.

Which socks do you like?   I like the striped ones.

striped   black   gray

plaid   gold   white

PRACTICE

Answer the questions with *one* or *ones*.

1. Which shoes do you like? (black) _I like the black ones._

2. Which shirt do you like? (striped) _____

3. Which pants do you like? (gray) _____

4. Which sweater do you like? (white) _____

5. Which earrings do you like? (gold) _____

6. Which hat do you like? (gray) _____

7. Which sneakers do you like?
   (white) _____

8. Which gloves do you like? (black) _____

9. Which jacket do you like? (plaid) _____

10. Which socks do you like? (striped) _____

11. Which watch do you like? (gold) _____

12. Which boots do you like? (black) _____

13. Which tie do you like? (plain) _____

14. Which shorts do you like? (white) _____

WHICH ONES DO YOU WANT?

Questions with *Which One* and *Which Ones*

Simple Present

 Which one do you want?   Which ones do you want?

PRACTICE

Make questions with *which one* or *which ones*.

1. Some grapes, please.   *Which ones do you want?*
2. A grapefruit, please.   _____
3. Some beans, please.   _____
4. Some potatoes, please.   _____
5. A pineapple, please.   _____
6. A watermelon, please.   _____
7. Some apples, please.   _____
8. A head of lettuce, please.   _____
9. A melon, please.   _____
10. Some tomatos, please.   _____
11. A cucumber, please.   _____
12. Some onions, please.   _____

MAKE IT WORK

Look at the picture. Then answer the question.

■ I want a pineapple, please.

☐ Which pineapple do you want?

■ _____

_____

I HARDLY EVER TAKE THE BUS.

Adverbs of Frequency

Simple Present

I	always / usually / often / sometimes	take the bus.
I	seldom / rarely / hardly ever / never	take the bus.

Note: Adverbs of frequency come before the main verb.
Seldom, rarely, hardly ever, and *never* express a negative idea.
Do not use these words with negative verbs.

PRACTICE

Make sentences with adverbs of frequency. Tell about yourself.

1. go to weddings   *I hardly ever go to weddings.*
2. write letters   _____
3. play cards   _____
4. read the newspaper   _____
5. go to concerts   _____
6. speak English at home   _____
7. have a headache   _____
8. eat breakfast in bed   _____
9. drink tea   _____
10. go to museums   _____
11. eat Chinese food   _____
12. get angry   _____
13. eat dinner at midnight   _____
14. sing in the shower   _____
15. eat spicy food   _____

New Word: spicy = containing a lot of spices such as pepper

DO YOU EVER PLAY CARDS?

Yes-No Questions with *Ever*

Simple Present

I never play chess.	He never reads books.
Do you ever play cards?	Does he ever read the newspaper?

PRACTICE

Make questions with *ever*.

1. I never drink soda. *Do you ever drink* _____ orange juice?

2. He never goes to plays. _____ to movies?

3. They never read books. _____ the newspaper?

4. She never cooks Chinese food. _____ Italian food?

5. They never go to baseball games. _____ to basketball games?

6. He never wears a tie. _____ a jacket?

7. I never play chess. _____ cards?

8. She never sleeps until noon. _____ until 10:00?

9. They never work on Sunday. _____ on Saturday?

10. He never takes a taxi. _____ a bus?

11. I never drink coffee. _____ tea?

12. She never goes to parties. _____ to weddings?

MAKE IT WORK

Write one question you would like to ask a classmate.

_____

58

I EXERCISE ONCE A DAY.

Adverbs

Simple Present

> How often do you exercise?
>
> I exercise | once | a day (week, month, year)
> | twice |
> | three times |
>
> I | never | exercise.

PRACTICE

Answer the questions.

1. How often do you wash your clothes?   *I wash my clothes once a week.*

2. How often do you iron your clothes?   _____

3. How often do you exercise?   _____

   _____

4. How often do you take a vacation?   _____

5. How often do you drink coffee?   _____

6. How often do you drink wine?   _____

7. How often do you take vitamins?   _____

8. How often do you catch a cold?   _____

9. How often do you go to the doctor?   _____

10. How often do you brush your teeth?   _____

MAKE IT WORK

Answer the questions about a classmate.

How often does he (or she) exercise? _____

How often does he (or she) get sick? _____

HOW OFTEN DOES SHE READ THE NEWSPAPER?

Questions with *How Often*

Simple Present

		She reads the newspaper.
How often	does	she read the newspaper?
		I play tennis.
How often	do you play tennis?	

PRACTICE

Make questions with *how often*.

1. I go to a gym. *How often do you go to a gym?*

2. They exercise. _____

3. He watches the news on TV. _____

4. I read the newspaper. _____

5. She visits her family. _____

6. They go to concerts. _____

7. He plays chess. _____

8. I go to the movies. _____

9. She plays tennis. _____

10. She goes to church. _____

11. They eat out. _____

12. I go to the beach. _____

MAKE IT WORK

Fill in the dialogue. Make questions with *how often*.

■ Do you eat out?

☐ Yes I do.

■ _____
_____?

☐ Oh, about twice a week.

■ What's your favorite restaurant?

☐ Pierre's French restaurant.

■ _____
_____?

☐ Once or twice a month.

SHE DRIVES CAREFULLY.

Adverbs of Manner

Simple Present

> She's a careful driver.   She drives careful ly.
>
> She's a good driver.   She drives well.
>
> Note: Add *ly* to form adverbs of manner.
>
> irregular adverbs: good → well   hard → hard   fast → fast

PRACTICE

Make sentences with adverbs of manner.

1. He's a careless driver.   *He drives carelessly.*

2. I'm a slow driver.   _____

3. He's a fast driver.   _____

4. They're quick learners.   _____

5. You're slow learners.   _____

6. I'm a good writer.   _____

7. She's a poor writer.   _____

8. We're quick readers.   _____

9. They're slow readers.   _____

10. He's a good dancer.   _____

11. She's a bad dancer.   _____

12. You're a careful worker.   _____

13. We're hard workers.   _____

14. He's a good tennis player.   _____

15. I'm a bad tennis player.   _____

MAKE IT WORK

Fill in the dialogue with a compliment.

■ You're a good dancer.

□ Really?

■ Absolutely. You _____

HE DOESN'T LIKE TO STAY HOME ON SATURDAY NIGHT.

Review: Present Tense, Verb + Infinitive, Adverbs

Chris Green

I spend Saturday night with my family. I usually stay home. I watch movies and talk to my son.

Oscar Hernandez

I work hard all week. I don't like to stay home on Saturday night. I need to talk to people. I want to talk about my week.

Anita Hug

I never miss the dance at Leisure World. I always have a ball.

Samantha Porter

I always have a date on Saturday night. I need to be with someone.

Mark Gunn

I don't plan my Saturday nights. I go to a bar or a party. I always have fun.

Linda Chan

I like to ride in my car with Pearl Jam on the radio. I sometimes rent a video and eat popcorn.

New Words: never miss = always go
              have a ball = have a good time

popcorn

HE DOESN'T LIKE TO STAY HOME ON SATURDAY NIGHT.

> I don't like to stay home on Saturday night.
>
> He doesn't like to stay home on Saturday night.

PRACTICE

Read page 62. Then make sentences about the people in the pictures. Change *I* to *he* or *she* and *my* to *his* or *her*.

1. Chris Green *spends Saturday night with his family.*
2. _____
3. _____
4. Oscar Hernandez _____
5. _____
6. _____
7. _____
8. Anita Hug _____
9. _____
10. Linda Chan _____
11. _____
12. Samantha Porter _____
13. _____
14. Mark Gunn _____
15. _____
16. _____

MAKE IT WORK

Answer the question.

What do you usually do on Saturday night?

_____

_____

WHAT DO YOU USUALLY DO ON THE WEEKEND?

Word Order: Statements, Questions, and Adverbs

Simple Present

WH word	first auxiliary	subject	auxiliary	adverb of frequency	main verb	object	adverb or adverb phrase
What	do	you		usually	do?		
		I			visit	my sister	once a week.
		I	don't		have	a lot of time.	
	Do	you		ever	watch	TV?	

PRACTICE

Put the words in the correct order.

Interviewer: 1. do / do / what / you / ?

What do you do?

Keiko: 2. architect / an / I'm / .

_____

3. buildings / design / I / .

_____

Interviewer: 4. you / what / in / do / free time / your / do / ?

_____

Keiko: 5. free time / don't / of / a / I / lot / have / .

_____

6. a / nights / week / I / take / class / a / three / .

_____

Interviewer: 7. you / do / what / the / on / do / weekend / usually / ?

_____

Keiko: 8. morning / work / on / I / Saturday / .

_____

             9. go / church / Sunday / usually / I / to / on / .

_____

Interviewer: 10. busy / very / you're / .

_____

Keiko: 11. am / yes, / I / .

_____

Interviewer: 12. you / ever / take / do / a / vacation / ?

_____

Keiko   13. a / Hawaii / once / go / I / year / to / .

_____

Interviewer: 14. do/ want / what / future / to / in / the / you / do / ?

_____

Keiko: 15. want / get / I / to / someday / married / .

_____

             16. children / to / I / want / have / .

_____

MAKE IT WORK

Rewrite the dialogue so that it is correct.

■ You do take a vacation ever?

■ _____

☐ Yes, but I no take usually a very long vacation.

☐ _____

Review: Simple Present, Verb *To Be*, Verb + Infinitive, Adverbs

	Keiko Goto	**Mary Ellen Spear**
Work	architect for the city of Tokyo	interior decorator for the city of Dallas, Texas
Food	soup, rice, fish, vegetables, and always hot tea with every meal	meat, potatoes, salad, vegetables, and a cup of coffee after every meal
Hobby	stamps	none
Family	single no children	married two children
Sports	golf	tennis
Clothes	suits, no bright colors at work	suits and dresses; never slacks at work
Entertainment	television news shows	movies
Vacations	Hawaii once a year	Mexico every winter

MARY ELLEN DOESN'T HAVE A HOBBY.

| Keiko | collects | stamps. |
| Mary Ellen | doesn't have | a hobby. |

PRACTICE

Read page 66. Then make sentences about Keiko Goto and Mary Ellen Spear.

Work

1. (be) Keiko Goto _is an architect._ _____

2. (work for) _____

3. (be) Mary Ellen Spear _____

4. (work for) _____

Food

5. (like to eat) Keiko _____

   _____

6. (drink) _____

   _____

7. (like to eat) Mary Ellen _____

   _____

8. (drink) _____

   _____

Hobby

9. (collect) Keiko _____

10. (not/have) Mary Ellen _____

Family

11. (be) Keiko _____

12. (not/have) _____

13. (be) Mary Ellen _____

14. (have) _____

MARY ELLEN DOESN'T HAVE A HOBBY.

Sports

15. (play) Keiko _____

16. (play) Mary Ellen _____

Clothes

17. (wear) Keiko _____

18. (not/wear) _____

19. (wear) Mary Ellen _____

20. (never/wear) _____

Entertainment

21. (like to watch) Keiko _____

22. (go) Mary Ellen _____

Vacations

23. (go) Keiko _____

24. (go) Mary Ellen _____

MAKE IT WORK

Make one sentence about yourself for each category.

Work   *I work, but I don't work in an office.* _____

_____

Food   _____

_____

Hobby   _____

Family   _____

_____

Sports   _____

Clothes   _____

_____

Entertainment   _____

_____

Vacations   _____

DO YOU LIKE TO EAT OUT? YES, I DO.

Contrast: Negative and Affirmative Short Answers

Simple Present, *There Is* **and** *There Are,* **Verb** *To Be*

Are there any good restaurants in your city?	Yes, there are.
Do you like to eat out?	Yes, I do.
Do you eat out often?	No, I don't.

PRACTICE

Answer the questions with short answers. Tell about yourself.

1. Do you like to read? _Yes, I do._

2. Is there a library in your town? _____

3. Are there any bookstores in your town? _____

4. Do you play the piano? _____

5. Do you like piano music? _____

6. Do you like to go to concerts? _____

7. Is there public transportation in your town? _____

8. Do you have a car? _____

9. Do you drive? _____

10. Are you a good driver? _____

11. Do you drive carefully? _____

12. Is there a public pool in your town? _____

13. Do you like to swim? _____

14. Are you a good swimmer? _____

15. Do you like sports? _____

16. Do you play tennis? _____

17. Are you a good tennis player? _____

18. Do you like to watch tennis games? _____

19. Do you have a hobby? _____

20. Do you collect anything? _____

HE'S SHORT, AND SHE IS TOO.

Contrast: Shortened Sentences with *And . . . Too*

Simple Present, Verb *To Be*

> He's short. She's short.   He likes dogs. She likes dogs.
>
> He's short, and she is too.   He likes dogs, and she does too.
>
> Note: Use *and* + auxiliary (*does, is*) + *too* to join two affirmative statements.

PRACTICE

Complete the sentences with *and . . . too*. Write about Nicole (she).

1. Bill is single, _and Nicole is too._____

2. He lives alone, _and she does too._____

3. He's intelligent, _____

4. He likes concerts, _____

5. He's very quiet, _____

6. He's always on time, _____

7. He likes to travel, _____

8. He likes to play golf, _____

9. He's an excellent golfer, _____

10. He's a good swimmer, _____

11. He's interested in sports, _____

12. He likes to read, _____

13. He has a good job, _____

14. He wants to get married, _____

MAKE IT WORK

Choose two sentences from above. Then write about yourself. Complete your sentences with *too*.

_Bill likes to travel , and I do too._____

_____

_____

SHE ISN'T VERY TALL, AND HE ISN'T EITHER.

Contrast: Shortened Sentences with *And . . . Either*

Simple Present, Verb *To Be*

> She isn't very tall. He isn't very tall.
> She isn't very tall, and he isn't either.
>
> She doesn't like to clean house. He doesn't like to clean house.
> She doesn't like to clean house, and he doesn't either.
>
> Note: Use *and* + auxiliary (*doesn't, isn't*) + *either* to join two negative
> statements.

PRACTICE

Complete the sentences with *and . . . either.* Write about Bill (he).

1. Nicole doesn't like big cities, *and Bill doesn't either.* _____

2. She isn't very talkative, _____

3. She doesn't like big parties, _____

4. She isn't a very good cook, _____

5. She doesn't like to clean house, _____

6. She isn't very neat, _____

7. She doesn't drink alcohol, _____

8. She doesn't smoke, _____

9. She doesn't like to eat out, _____

10. She doesn't have a lot of money, _____

11. She isn't a very good dancer, _____

12. She doesn't like rock music, _____

13. She isn't very tall, _____

14. She doesn't watch TV very often,_____

MAKE IT WORK

Choose two sentences from above. Then write about yourself. Complete
your sentences with *either.*

She isn't a very good dancer, and I'm not either. _____

_____

_____

CATS DON'T OBEY, BUT DOGS DO.

Contrast: Shortened Sentences with *But*

Simple Present, Verb *To Be*

affirmative	negative
Cats wash themselves,	but dogs don't.
Cats are independent,	but dogs aren't.

negative	affirmative
Cats don't obey,	but dogs do.
Cats aren't very friendly,	but dogs are.

Note: Use *but* to join affirmative and negative statements.

PRACTICE

Complete the sentences with *but*. Write about dogs.

1. Cats are independent, *but dogs aren't.* _____

2. Cats aren't very friendly, _____

3. Cats don't need a lot of attention, _____

4. Cats are easy to care for, _____

5. Cats wash themselves, _____

6. Cats aren't expensive to feed, _____

7. Cats don't obey, _____

8. Cats scratch people, _____

9. Cats catch mice, _____

10. Cats see well at night, _____

11. Cats don't like water, _____

12. Cats like to climb trees, _____

13. Cats prefer to eat fish, _____

14. Cats have nine lives, _____

New Words: independent = not dependent
care for = take care of, look after
obey = follow a command

irregular plural: mouse = mice

YOU WON'T CHANGE JOBS NEXT YEAR, AND I WON'T EITHER.

Contrast: Shortened Sentences with *Too*, *Either*, and *But*

Simple Present, Verb *To Be*, Present Continuous, Future

You'll probably buy a new house next year,	and I will too.
You won't change jobs next year,	and I won't either.
You play tennis,	but I don't.
You don't speak Spanish,	but I do.

Note: Put a comma before *and* and *but*.

PRACTICE

Write about yourself. Finish your sentences with *too*, *either*, or *but*.

1. I'm from the United States.

   You're from the United States, but I'm not.

2. I live in California.

   _____

3. I'm married.

   _____

4. I'm a teacher.

   _____

5. I'll probably retire in ten years.

   _____

6. I like to travel.

   _____

7. I'm going to go to Spain next summer.

   _____

8. I don't speak Spanish.

   _____

9. I'm taking Spanish lessons now.

   _____

10. I'm not a very good cook.

    _____

I DIRECT MOVIES. I'M DIRECTING A COMEDY NOW.

Contrast: Simple Present, Verb *To Be*, Present Continuous

> I ▢direct▢ movies. I ▢'m▢ a movie director.
> I ▢'m directing▢ a comedy now.

PRACTICE

Fill in the blanks with the correct tense. Use the verbs below.

| be | design | decorate | play | write | paint | act |

1. I *'m*_____ an interior decorator. I _decorate_____ people's houses.
   At the moment, I _____ a movie star's house in Hollywood.

2. They _____ musicians. They _____ the guitar.
   Currently, they _____ at a nighclub in Dallas.

3. She _____ books. She _____ a writer. She ____
   _____ a book about travel in Spain right now.

4. He _____ an artist. He _____ pictures. He ____
   _____ a picture of the president now.

5. They _____ actors. They usually _____ in movies, but
   right now they _____ in a television commercial.

6. I _____ an architect. Right now I _____ an office
   building in New York. I usually _____ houses, but I also
   _____ office buildings.

MAKE IT WORK

Complete the dialogue.

☐ What do you do?

■ _____ _____

☐ And what are you doing at the moment?

■ _____

DO YOU HAVE ANYTHING CHEAPER?

Adjective Comparatives with *-er*

Simple Present

short–short er   cheap–cheap er   wide–wide r

Note: Add *er* or *r* to most one-syllable adjectives.

adjective opposites: expensive–cheap   narrow–wide   short–long

heavy–light   high–low   small–large

tight–loose   dull–sharp

PRACTICE

Ask questions with an adjective opposite. Be sure to add *er* or *r* to the adjective.

1.   This watch is too expensive.   *Do you have anything cheaper?*

2.   This tie is too narrow.   _____

3.   This belt is too long.   _____

4.   This jacket is too short.   _____

5.   These gloves are too large.   _____

6.   The heels of these shoes are too low.   _____

7.   These pants are too loose.   _____

8.   This T-shirt is too small.   _____

9.   This knife is too dull.   _____

10.   This purse is too large.   _____

11.   This sweater is too tight.   _____

12   This wallet is too expensive.   _____

13.   These shoes are too narrow.   _____

14.   This coat is too heavy.   _____

15.   The heels of these shoes are

too high.   _____

BETTY IS PRETTIER THAN HER SISTER.

Spelling: Adjective Comparatives
Verb *To Be*

> Betty is prett[ier] than her sister.   Betty is fat[ter] than her sister
>
> Note: When you are comparing two things or two people, follow these
> rules: If an adjective ends in *y*, change the *y* to *i* and add *er*.
> pretty → prett i e r. If an adjective ends in one vowel + one
> consonant, double the consonant before adding *er*: f a t → fa t t er.

PRACTICE

Make sentences with the correct comparative form.

1. Betty is happy. Bob is very happy.
    Bob is happier than Betty.

2. Susan is very thin. Joe is thin.

    _____

3. Jenny is very old. Her sister is old.

    _____

4. Polly is heavy. Molly is very heavy.

    _____

5. Paul is very tall. Laura is tall.

    _____

6. Ed is fat. Ron is very fat.

    _____

7. Diane is very pretty. Her sister is pretty.

    _____

8. The secretary is very smart. Her boss is smart.

    _____

9. Dave is noisy. Philip is very noisy.

    _____

10. Mike is very messy. His secretary is messy.

    _____

MAKE IT WORK

Compare yourself to a brother or sister.

_____

_____

A SPORTS CAR IS MORE EXPENSIVE THAN A STATION WAGON.

Adjective Comparatives with *More*

Verb *To Be*, Simple Present

a sports car   **a station wagon**

A sports car is | more expensive than | a station wagon.
A sports car is | more powerful than | a station wagon.

Note: When you are comparing two people or two things, put *more*
before adjectives with three or more syllables:
ex • pen • sive (three syllables) = more expensive

PRACTICE

Fill in the blanks with the correct comparative form.

A sports car is *more luxurious than* _____ a station wagon.
(1. luxurious)

It's _____ a station wagon too. It's also
(2. elegant)

_____ a station wagon. It can go 120 miles per hour
(3. beautiful)

and is _____ a station wagon. It gets good gasoline
(4. powerful)

mileage, so it's _____ a station wagon. However, it's
(5. economical)

_____ a station wagon. It can cost $40,000.
(6. expensive)

A station wagon is _____ a sports car. It's
(7. popular)

_____ a sports car. It has large seats and is
(8. practical)

_____ a sports car. And a station wagon is
(9. comfortable)

_____ a sports car.
(10. cheap)

Equivalents: mile = 1.6 kilometers

THE GRAY HOUSE IS MORE MODERN.

Adjective Comparatives with *-er* and *More*
Verb *To Be*

> The gray house is | larger.
> The gray house is | more modern.

Note: Put *more* before two-syllable adjectives:
      modern, charming: more modern, more charming

      irregular comparative form: good → better

PRACTICE

Fill in the blanks with the correct comparative form.

	the white house	the gray house
size	5 rooms	7 rooms
age	80 years old	4 years old
cost	$200,000	$325,000
taxes	$1,532	$4,100

The white house is _smaller_ (1. small). It's _____ (2. old). It's
also _____ (3. charming). It's _____ (4. cheap). The taxes are
_____ (5. low). The garage is _____ (6. big), but the yard is
_____ (7. small).

The gray house is _____ (8. large). It's also _____ (9. expensive).
It's _____ (10. modern). The garage is _____ (11. small). The yard
is _____ (12. large), and the taxes are _____ (13. high). The
gray house is _____ (14. elegant). It's also in a _____ (15. good)
neighborhood.

New Word: taxes = money homeowners or landowners owe to the town or
              city they live in

78

DONNA IS THE OLDEST.

Adjective Superlatives with -est

Verb *To Be*

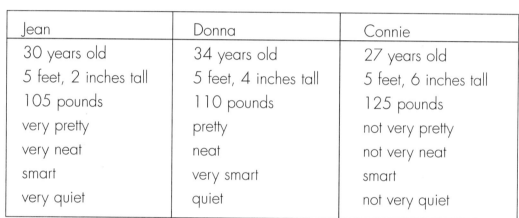

Donna is | the oldest.

Jean is | the prettiest.

Note: When you are comparing three or more people or things, add *est* to most one-syllable adjectives.
When a two-syllable adjective ends in *y*, change the *y* to *i* and add *est*.

PRACTICE

Look at the chart below. Then make superlative sentences about Jean, Donna, and Connie.

Jean	Donna	Connie
30 years old	34 years old	27 years old
5 feet, 2 inches tall	5 feet, 4 inches tall	5 feet, 6 inches tall
105 pounds	110 pounds	125 pounds
very pretty	pretty	not very pretty
very neat	neat	not very neat
smart	very smart	smart
very quiet	quiet	not very quiet

1. quiet   *Jean is the quietest.*
2. old _____
3. young _____
4. tall _____
5. short _____
6. heavy _____
7. light _____
8. pretty _____
9. neat _____
10. smart _____

Equivalents: 1 foot = 30.5 centimeters   1 inch = 2.54 centimeters
1 pound = .45 kilograms

GOLD IS THE MOST VALUABLE.

Adjective Superlatives with *The Most*

Verb *To Be*

Gold, silver, and copper are all valuable.

Gold is the most valuable.

Concerts, ballets, and movies are all interesting.

Movies are the most interesting.

Note: When you are comparing three or more people or things, put *the most* before adjectives with three or more syllables. Put *the most* before the adjectives *harmful* and *famous*.

singular: coffee is   plural: movies are

PRACTICE

Make sentences with *the most*. Express your own opinion.

1. Wine, cigarettes, and coffee are all harmful.

   Cigarettes are the most harmful.

2. Basketball, soccer, and football are all exciting.

   _____

3. Dogs, cats, and horses are all intelligent.

   _____

4. Italian food, Chinese food, and French food are all delicious.

   _____

5. Gold, silver, and copper are all valuable.

   _____

6. Fords, Cadillacs, and Volkswagens are all popular.

   _____

7. Nylon, cotton, and polyester are all practical.

   _____

8. Concerts, ballets, and movies are all interesting.

   _____

9. Photographs, drawings, and paintings are all beautiful.

   _____

10. Paula Abdul, Madonna, and Whitney Houston are all famous.

    _____

NEWARK IS THE LARGEST CITY IN NEW JERSEY.

Adjective Superlatives with -est and The Most

Verb To Be, Simple Present

Newark is the largest city in New Jersey.

Newark is the most important city in New Jersey.

Note: When comparing three or more things, add *est* to one-syllable adjectives; put *the most* before adjectives of two or more syllables. Some two-syllable words have two forms:

lovely → loveliest (or) most lovely

busy → busiest (or) most busy

irregular superlative form: good → best.

PRACTICE

Fill in the blanks with the correct superlative form.

1. (large) Newark is _the largest_____ city in New Jersey.

2. (old) Trenton is one of _____ cities.

3. (modern) Newark is probably _____ city.

4. (busy) Newark has one of _____ airports in the country.

5. (important) Newark is _____ city in New Jersey.

6. (popular) Atlantic City is _____ resort in the state.

7. (rich) Princeton is probably _____ city in New Jersey.

8. (large) Rutgers State University is _____ university in the state.

9. (long) The Delaware is _____ river in New Jersey.

10. (important) Tomatoes and corn are _____ crops.

11. (good) The Trenton Museum is one of _____ museums in New Jersey.

12. (beautiful) Cape May is probably _____ city in New Jersey.

MAKE IT WORK

Tell about your state or country.

_____ is the largest city in _____

_____

BASEBALL IS THE MOST POPULAR.

Review: Comparatives and Superlatives

Verb *To Be*

> Concerts and movies are both popular forms of entertainment.
>
> Movies are more popular.
>
> Baseball, golf, and tennis are all popular sports.
>
> Baseball is the most popular.

PRACTICE

Make comparative or superlative sentences. Express your own opinion.

1. *Gone With the Wind* and *Casablanca* are both interesting movies.

   Casablanca is more interesting.

2. Tennis, baseball, and soccer are all exciting sports.

   _____

3. Skiing and golf are both expensive sports.

   _____

4. Madonna and Cher are both good singers.

   _____

5. Concerts, ballet, movies, and TV are all popular forms of entertainment.

   _____

6. Talk shows, game shows, and comedies are all interesting TV programs.

   _____

7. Disneyland and Eurodisney are both large amusement parks.

   _____

8. Tom Cruise, Tom Hanks, and Michael Douglas are all good actors.

   _____

9. Photographs and painting are both beautiful.

   _____

10. Chess and checkers are both popular games.

   _____

New Word: checkers

COOK ONE POUND OF GREEN BEANS.

Affirmative Imperatives

She cooks one pound of green beans.
Cook one pound of green beans.

She washes the beans.

She cuts the ends off the beans.

She boils two cups of water.

She adds the beans.

She cooks them.

She drains the water off.

She puts the beans on a plate.

She puts butter on top.

She serves them.

PRACTICE

Look at the pictures above. Then tell someone how to cook green beans.

1. _Wash the beans._
2. _____
3. _____
4. _____
5. _____
6. _____
7. _____
8. _____
9. _____

MAKE IT WORK

Fill in the blanks with an imperative. Use the verbs from the Practice above.

How to Cook Spaghetti

1. _____ six quarts of water.

2. _____ the spaghetti to the boiling water.

3. _____ it for 10-12 minutes.

4. _____ the water off.

5. _____ it hot.

WOULD YOU PLEASE CLOSE THE DOOR?

Polite Requests with *Would*

Close the door.
Please close the door.
| Would you please close | the door?

Note: Use *Would you please* when you want to make a polite request.

PRACTICE

Fill in the blanks with a polite request. Use these words below.

turn   answer   close   open

1. The radio is loud.   *Would you please turn* _____ it down?

2. The door is open.   _____ it?

3. The oven is on.   _____ it off?

4. The telephone is ringing.   _____ it?

5. The window is closed.   _____ it?

6. The water is running.   _____ it off?

7. The light is on.   _____ it off?

8. The doorbell is ringing.   _____ the door?

9. The sound is too low.   _____ it up?

10. The computer is off.   _____ it on?

11. The drawer is open.   _____ it?

12. The food is burning.   _____ the stove
down?

MAKE IT WORK

You are in a movie theater. Make one polite request for each situation.

The woman in front of you is wearing a large hat.

_____ off your hat?

The man next to her is standing up.

_____ down?

The people behind you are talking.

_____ quiet?

84

MAY I USE THE TELEPHONE?

Requests for Permission with *Can* and *May*

Can I use the telephone?   May I use the telephone?

Note: Use *can* or *may* to make requests for permission. *Can* is used for informal situations; *may* is used for more formal situations.

PRACTICE

Read each situation and ask for permission.

1. You are in class. You want to borrow a classmate's dictionary.
   Can I borrow your dictionary?

2. You are on the telephone. You want to speak to Dr. Lau.
   _____

3. You are standing outside your boss's office. You want to come in.
   _____

4. You are at a friend's house. You want to use the telephone.
   _____

5. You are talking to your boss. You want to leave work early today.
   _____

6. You are with a classmate. You want to borrow a dollar.
   _____

7. You are in class. You want to ask the teacher a question.
   _____

8. You are with a classmate in class. You want to have a piece of paper.
   _____

9. You are at a friend's house. You want to use the bathroom.
   _____

10. You are a clerk in a department store. You want to help a customer.
    _____

LET'S GO TO THE MOVIES.

Suggestions with *Let's*

> Why don't we go to the movies?
>
> | Let's go | to the movies.
>
> Note: *Let's* is a suggestion that includes both the speaker and the listener.

PRACTICE

Make new sentences with *Let's*.

1. Why don't we watch television?   *Let's watch television.* _____
2. Why don't we dance?   _____
3. Why don't we eat out?   _____
4. Why don't we go to the movies?   _____
5. Why don't we listen to music?   _____
6. Why don't we go to a soccer game?   _____
7. Why don't we play cards?   _____
8. Why don't we go to the park?   _____
9. Why don't we play tennis?   _____
10. Why don't we go to a concert?   _____
11. Why don't we rent a video?   _____
12. Why don't we go for a walk?   _____
13. Why don't we have a party?   _____
14. Why don't we stay home?   _____

MAKE IT WORK

It is Saturday evening. You and a friend are bored. Suggest three things to do.

Let's play miniature golf. _____

_____

_____

_____

LET'S GO BY BUS.

Prepositional Phrases with *By*

Suggestions with *Let's*

Let's go | by | car.
bus.
taxi.
subway.
train.
boat.
plane.

Note: After *by*, do not use *a*, *an*, or *the*.

PRACTICE

Read each pair of sentences. Decide which is the faster way to travel. Then make sentences with *by*.

1. The bus leaves at 3:00.
   The train leaves at 2:30.   *Let's go by train.*

2. The boat takes five days.
   The plane takes ten hours.

3. The subway takes an hour.
   A taxi takes forty minutes.

4. The train leaves every hour.
   The bus leaves every half hour.

5. The plane takes one hour.
   The train takes eight hours.

6. The bus takes twenty minutes.
   A taxi takes five minutes.

7. The train takes two hours.
   A car takes an hour.

8. The boat takes two days.
   The plane takes two hours.

9. The train is usually on time.
   The bus is always late.

10. The subway comes every ten
    minutes. The bus comes every
    twenty-five minutes.

87

LET'S NOT GO BY BUS.

Negative Suggestions with _Let's_

Let's go by bus.	Let's not go | by bus.
Let's go by taxi.	Let's not go | by taxi.
Let's go by subway.	Let's not go | by subway.

 PRACTICE

Make negative sentences with _Let's_.

1. Gasoline is expensive. _Let's not go by car._

2. The bus is too slow. _____

3. A taxi is too expensive. _____

4. The train takes a long time. _____

5. The ferry is always late. _____

6. The boat takes too long. _____

7. The train is expensive. _____

8. The bus takes an hour. _____

9. The car is in bad condition. _____

10. The plane is too expensive. _____

11. The subway is too crowded. _____

12. The bus is never on time. _____

MAKE IT WORK

You and a friend are going to go to the movies. Read your friend's suggestions Then make negative suggestions with _Let's_ and explain why.

Let's go by train. _Let's not go by train._

It takes too long.

Let's go by taxi. _____

_____

Let's go by bus. _____

_____

YOU SHOULD BE ON TIME.

Advice with *Should* and *Shouldn't*

You [should be] on time.   You [shouldn't be] late.

Note: Use *should* plus the simple form of the verb for advice.

contraction: shouldn't = should not

PRACTICE

Make negative or affirmative sentences with *should*. Begin your sentences with *You*. Use contractions whenever possible.

1. be on time for a job interview   *You should be on time for a job interview*.

2. be late   _____

3. dress neatly   _____

4. wear flashy clothes   _____

5. speak clearly   _____

6. chew gum   _____

7. be polite   _____

8. look at the interviewer   _____

9. sit up straight   _____

10. smoke   _____

11. answer the interviewer's

    questions   _____

12. thank the interviewer for his

    or her time   _____

MAKE IT WORK

Look at the picture. This boy is at a job interview. Give him some advice.

He should sit up straight.

_____

_____

_____

YOU CAN DRIVE ACROSS THE GOLDEN GATE BRIDGE.

Possibility with *Can*

> You can drive across the Golden Gate Bridge.
>
> Note: Use *can* to express possibility.

PRACTICE

Name some things you can do on a vacation in San Francisco. Begin your sentences with *You*.

cable car

Come to San Francisco!

Ride the cable cars. Drive across the Golden Gate Bridge. See Fisherman's Wharf. Eat fantastic seafood. Go to Chinatown, the "city within a city." Take a boat tour of San Francisco Bay. Go to North Beach. Walk in Golden Gate Park. Visit the beautiful city of Carmel. And don't miss the sea lions at Seal Rock.

sea lion

1. *You can ride the cable cars.* _____
2. _____
3. _____
4. _____
5. _____
6. _____
7. _____
8. _____
9. _____
10. _____

MAKE IT WORK

Name three things you can do on a vacation in or near your city.

_____

_____

_____

WHERE CAN YOU GET A CUP OF COFFEE AROUND HERE?

Questions with *Where*, Impersonal Pronoun *You*
Possibility with *Can*

> | Where | can | you | get a cup of coffee around here?
> | You | can get a cup of coffee at a coffee shop.
>
> Note: Use *you* to make general statements. you = any person.

a coffee shop　　**a drug store**　　**a newsstand**　　**a gas station**　　**a bank**

PRACTICE

Ask questions with *where*. Then look at the pictures above and answer your questions. Be sure to use *you* in both your question and your answer.

1. a cup of coffee　　*Where can you get a cup of coffee?*
　　　　　　　　　　You can get a cup of coffee at a coffee shop.

2. a magazine　　_____

3. some traveler's checks　　_____

4. some medicine　　_____

5. some gum　　_____

6. a newspaper　　_____

7. a hamburger　　_____

8. some gasoline　　_____

Negative Statements with *Can't*

> You [can't smoke] in the restaurant.
>
> Note: can't = not permitted; not allowed
> contraction: can't = cannot

PRACTICE

Tell what these signs mean. Make negative sentences with *You can't.*

1. *You can't smoke*

in the restaurant.

2. _____

the water.

3. _____

your bicycle in the park.

4. _____

alcohol on the beach.

5. _____

your dog in the store.

6. _____

on the grass.

THEY'D LIKE SOME HELP.

Affirmative Statements with *Would Like*

> I
> You
> He ['d like] some help.
> She
> We
> They
>
> Note: Use *would like* to talk about what a person wants (a preference).
>
> contraction: I'd = I would

PRACTICE

Make sentences with *would like*. Use one of these endings in your sentences:

some water	some rest
some company	some money
some help	some dry clothes
some food	a sweater
some medicine	a map

1. I'm thirsty.   *I'd like some water.*

2. Brian and Chris are in trouble. _____

3. Mark is cold.   _____

4. Art is hungry.   _____

5. I'm tired.   _____

6. Anita and Kathy are sick.   _____

7. John is broke.   _____

8. They're lost.   _____

9. We're wet.   _____

10. Kathy is lonely.   _____

MAKE IT WORK

Answer the questions.

When is your birthday?   _____

What would you like for your

next birthday?   _____

New Word: broke = having no money

WOULD YOU LIKE A COUGH DROP?

Yes-No Questions with *Would Like*

> I'm cold.
> Would you like a sweater?

PRACTICE

Make questions with *would like*.

1. I'm thirsty. (some soda)   *Would you like some soda?*

2. They're hungry. (some cake)   _____

3. I'm cold. (a blanket)   _____

4. She's hot. (some cold water)   _____

5. We're wet. (some dry clothes)   _____

6. I'm bored. (a good book)   _____

7. We're sleepy. (some coffee)   _____

8. He's sick. (some medicine)   _____

9. I'm lost. (some directions)   _____

10. He's broke. (some money)   _____

11. They're in trouble. (some help) _____

12. She's lonely. (some company)   _____

13. He's thirsty. (some water)   _____

14. I'm hungry. (a hamburger)   _____

15. We're lost. (a map)   _____

MAKE IT WORK

Offer one of the items on the right.

I have a sore throat.   *Would you like* _____

I have a headache.   _____

I cut my finger.   _____

94

WOULD YOU LIKE TO GO SWIMMING?

Go + Complement
Invitations with *Would like*

> Would you like to | go swimming?
> go fishing?
> go sailing?
>
> Note: Use *would like* to invite someone to do something.

PRACTICE

Make questions with *would like*.

1. fishing — *Would you like to go fishing?*
2. skiing — _____
3. sailing — _____
4. swimming — _____
5. ice-skating — _____
6. horseback riding — _____
7. bowling — _____
8. camping — _____
9. jogging — _____
10. bicycle riding — _____

MAKE IT WORK

Look at the dialogue. Then invite a friend to go shopping.

■ Would you like to go jogging today? ■ _____

☐ Sure. That sounds like fun.   ☐ Sure. That sounds like fun.

New Words:

horseback riding   bowling   sailing   jogging

I HAVE TO WRITE A REPORT.

Affirmative Statements with *Have To*

I You We They	can't go to the party.	I You We They	have to write a report.
He She		He She	has to write a report.

Note: Use *have to* to express necessity or obligation

PRACTICE

Make sentences with *have to* or *has to*.

1. She can't go. (study)   *She has to study.*

2. He can't go. (work)   _____

3. I can't go. (wash my hair)   _____

4. You can't go. (clean the house)   _____

5. She can't go. (wash her clothes)   _____

6. He can't go. (write some letters)   _____

7. We can't go. (visit our parents)   _____

8. They can't go. (go to a meeting)   _____

9. He can't go. (write a report)   _____

10. I can't go. (go to bed early)   _____

11. She can't go. (babysit)   _____

12. They can't go. (study)   _____

13. You can't go. (practice the piano)   _____

14. I can't go. (go to the doctor)   _____

MAKE IT WORK

Look at the dialogue. Then refuse your friend's invitation.

☐ Would you like to go shopping?   ☐ Would you like to go bowling?

■ Sorry, I can't. I have to study.   ■ _____

_____

SHE DOESN'T HAVE TO GET UP EARLY.

Negative Statements with *Have To*

I You We They	don't have to get	up early.	He She	doesn't have to get	up early.

Note: don't/doesn't have to = not necessary

PRACTICE

Make negative sentences about Gloria when she's on vacation.

When Gloria isn't on vacation:

1. She has to get up early.
2. She has to go to bed early.
3. She has to go to work.
4. She has to be on time.
5. She has to cook.
6. She has to do the dishes.
7. She has to do her homework.
8. She has to clean the house.
9. She has to iron her clothes.
10. She has to wash her clothes.
11. She has to work in the yard.
12. She has to feed the cat.

When Gloria's on vacation:

1. *She doesn't have to get up early.*
2. _____
3. _____
4. _____
5. _____
6. _____
7. _____
8. _____
9. _____
10. _____
11. _____
12. _____

MAKE IT WORK

Name three things you don't have to do when you're on vacation.

I don't have to cook.

_____

_____

_____

DO YOU HAVE TO TAKE A TEST?

Yes-No Questions with *Have To*

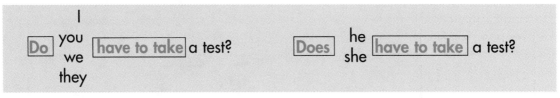

[Do] I you we they [have to take] a test?   [Does] he she [have to take] a test?

PRACTICE

Make questions with *have to*.

Barbara wants to get a job as a computer programmer.

1. (fill out an application)   *Does she have to fill out an application?*
   _____

2. (have an interview)   _____
   _____

I want to get a driver's license.

3. (fill out an application)   _____
   _____

4. (take a written test)   _____
   _____

5. (take a driving test)   _____
   _____

Bob and Florie want to open a bank account.

6. (deposit some money in the bank)   _____
   _____

7. (fill out a form)   _____
   _____

8. (sign their names)   _____
   _____

Brian wants to cash a check.

9. (endorse the check)   _____
   _____

10. (show his driver's license)   _____
    _____

New Words: deposit = put money in the bank
  endorse = sign a name on the back of a check
  application = a form to be filled out

Have To vs. Can and Can't

You can drive 45 miles an hour, but you can't drive over 55. You have to obey the speed limit.

Note: have to = necessary
     can = possible
     can't = not permitted; not allowed

Do not use *to* after *can*.

PRACTICE

Look at the signs and labels. Fill in the blanks with *have to, can,* or *can't.*

1. You <u>can</u> park here, but you <u>have to</u> put 25¢ in the meter.

2. You _____ have 75¢ change. You _____ give the driver three quarters or seven dimes and a nickel.

Please Take a Number To Be Served

3. You _____ take a number if you want someone to help you. Then you _____ wait until your number is called.

Joe's Bar
No One Under 21 Admitted

4. You _____ be 21 years old to get into Joe's Bar. You _____ be older than 21, but you _____ be younger than 21.

Proper I.D. Required
To Cash a Check

5. You _____ show an identification card to cash a check. You _____ use a driver's license or a passport.

6. You _____ take a tablet every four hours. You _____ take more than four tablets a day.

7. You _____ use this door. You _____ use the door on Main Street.

8. You _____ wash the sweater by hand. You _____ take it to the dry cleaners.

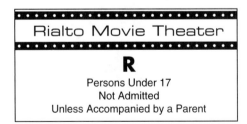

9. You _____ park here, but you _____ park for longer than 20 minutes.

10. You _____ see the movie if you are 17 years old. If you are 16 years old, your parents _____ be with you.

100

WOULD YOU LIKE TO GO TO THE MOVIES?

Review: Modals, Idiomatic Modals, and Requests

an invitation	**Would you like to go** to the movies?
a suggestion	**Let's go** to the movies.
an obligation	Sorry. I **have to study.**
a preference	I **'d like to see** the new Clint Eastwood movie.
a polite request	**Would you please call** the theater for movie times?
advice	We **should be** on time for the movie.
possibility	We **can buy** some popcorn or candy at the theater.
permission	**Can (or May) I borrow** $7.00 for the movie?

PRACTICE

Read each situation and make an appropriate response.

1. You want to get some pizza after class. Invite a classmate to go with you.

    Would you like to get some pizza after class?

2. You are at a coffee shop. The waitress takes your order. Order a cup of coffee.

    _____

3. A friend invites you to go swimming. You have to go to the doctor. Refuse your friend's invitation.

    _____

    _____

4. Your friend falls down and hurts his leg. You want him to go to the doctor. Give him some advice.

    _____

    _____

5. You and a friend want to go to a movie. Suggest that you and your friend go to the early show.

    _____

6. You want to go shopping Saturday. Invite a friend to go with you.

_____

7. You are in a movie theater. The man in front of you is standing up.
   Ask the man to sit down. Be polite.

_____

8. You are at work. You have an appointment with the doctor in the
   afternoon. Ask your boss for permission to leave work early.

_____

_____

9. You and a friend are watching TV at your friend's house. The
   sound is too low. You can't hear very well. Ask your friend to turn the
   sound up.

_____

_____

10. Look at the picture of the vending machine. You have three quarters.
    Tell what items you can buy.

_____

_____

THERE WERE SOME BOOKS ON THE TABLE A FEW MINUTES AGO.

There Was and *There Were*

| I can't find my book. | There was | a book on the table a few minutes ago. |
| I can't find my books. | There were | some books on the table a few minutes ago. |

PRACTICE

Make sentences with *there* was or *there* were.

1. I can't find my umbrella.

   There was an umbrella on the table a few minutes ago.

2. I can't find my gloves.

   _____

3. I can't find my keys.

   _____

4. I can't find my purse.

   _____

5. I can't find my glasses.

   _____

6. I can't find my checkbook.

   _____

7. I can't find my credit cards.

   _____

8. I can't find my wallet.

   _____

9. I can't find my camera.

   _____

10. I can't find my matches.

    _____

MAKE IT WORK

Complete the dialogue with *there was* or *there were*.

☐ Where are my credit cards? I can't find them anywhere.

■ _____

THERE WASN'T ANY PUBLIC TRANSPORTATION.

There Wasn't and *There Weren't*

| There weren't | any buses in the town. |
| There wasn't | any public transportation. |

Note: Use *there wasn't* with uncountable nouns
electricity   transportation   water   heat   service
contractions: wasn't = was not   weren't = were not

PRACTICE

Last winter there was a terrible snowstorm in Pennsylvania. The town of New Hope had nine feet of snow. Because of the snowstorm, everything in the town stopped.

Tell about the town. Make sentences with *there wasn't* or *there weren't*.

1. cars on the road   _There weren't any cars on the road._

2. food deliveries   _____

3. mail deliveries   _____

4. telephone service   _____

5. people on the street   _____

6. electricity   _____

7. lights in the town   _____

8. elevators working   _____

9. heat   _____

10. hot water   _____

MAKE IT WORK

Tell about a terrible snowstorm, rainstorm, or windstorm in your town or city.

There was a terrible _____

Because of the storm, there wasn't _____

_____

New Words: delivery   electricity   heat

SHE EMPTIED THE WASTEPAPER BASKETS.

Spelling: *-d, -ed, -ied*

Simple Past

–d	–ed	–ied
change → change[d]	clean → clean[ed]	empty → empt[ied]

Note: Add *d* or *ed* to form the regular past tense.
If a verb ends in *y* and there is a consonant before the *y*, change the *y* to *i* and then add *ed*: try → tried.

PRACTICE

Read what Mrs. Gross does every Saturday. Then rewrite the sentences. Tell about Mrs. Gross's day last Saturday. Change the sentences to the past tense.

Mrs. Gross does all of her work every Saturday. She fixes breakfast at 7:00. After breakfast she washes the dishes. Then she dries them. In the morning she cleans the house. She vacuums the rug, and she dusts the furniture. She empties the wastepaper baskets. Then she carries out the trash. In the afternoon she washes the clothes. Then she folds them. She also changes the bed. Then she irons. At 4:00 she shops for food. And, of course, she cooks dinner at 6:00.

Mrs. Gross did all of her work last Saturday.
_____
_____
_____
_____
_____
_____
_____
_____
_____
_____
_____

I PAID MY BILLS TWO WEEKS AGO.

Irregular Past Tense Verbs

When did you last pay your bills? I paid my bills two weeks ago.

last night.

a month ago.

pay → paid	read → read	send → sent	buy → bought
say → said	lose → lost	leave → left	think → thought
	see → saw	feel → felt	get → got
take → took	meet → met		forget → forgot

PRACTICE

Answer the questions. Tell about yourself.

1. When did you last pay your bills?   *I paid my bills a week ago.*

2. When did you last say something silly?   _____

3. When did you last meet someone new?   _____

4. When did you last leave a party   _____
    at midnight?   _____

5. When did you last read a newspaper?   _____

6. When did you last lose something?   _____

7. When did you last see a good movie?   _____

8. When did you last take a taxi?   _____

9. When did you last feel sick?   _____

10. When did you last get angry?   _____

11. When did you last send a package?   _____

12. When did you last buy a book?   _____

13. When did you last forget an   _____
     appointment?   _____

14. When did you last think about   _____
     your family?   _____

I WENT TO THE DOCTOR YESTERDAY.

Irregular Past Tense Verbs

When did you last go to the doctor? I | went | to the doctor yesterday.

a week ago.

three months ago.

eat → ate	make → made	break → broke	cut → cut
give → gave	have → had	write → wrote	put → put
drink → drank	wear → wore	speak → spoke	hurt → hurt
	tear → tore	drive → drove	go → went

PRACTICE

Answer the questions. Tell about yourself.

1. When did you last eat Chinese food?   *I ate Chinese food two weeks ago.*

2. When did you last give a party?   _____

3. When did you last make a phone call?   _____

4. When did you last have a headache?   _____

5. When did you last break something?   _____

6. When did you last drive a car?   _____

7. When did you last hurt your back?   _____

8. When did you last write a letter?   _____

9. When did you last speak to your
    neighbor?   _____
    _____

10. When did you last cut your finger?   _____

11. When did you last put on
     something red?   _____
     _____

12. When did you last drink wine?   _____

13. When did you last go to the doctor?   _____

14. When did you last wear blue jeans?   _____

15. When did you last tear your clothes?   _____

I LOST MY KEYS. HE LOST HIS TOO.

Possessive Pronouns

Regular and Irregular Past Tense Verbs

I lost my keys.	I lost	mine	too.
	You lost	yours	too.
	He lost	his	too.
	She lost	hers	too.
	We lost	ours	too.
	They lost	theirs	too.

Note: **subject pronoun   possessive pronoun**
I   mine

PRACTICE

Make sentences with possessive pronouns.

1. I lost my keys.   He   _lost his too._
2. I broke my glasses.   You   _____
3. I cut my finger.   She   _____
4. I drove my car.   You   _____
5. I took my camera.   They _____
6. I forgot my checkbook.   He   _____
7. I found my credit cards. We   _____
8. I carried my umbrella.   I   _____
9. I broke my watch.   She   _____
10. I wore my coat.   You   _____
11. I took my briefcase.   I   _____
12. I lost my suitcase.   They _____
13. I hurt my back.   He   _____
14. I forgot my scarf.   She   _____
15. I paid my bills.   We   _____
16. I cut my hair.   I   _____

DO YOU WANT TO BORROW MINE?

Possessive Adjectives vs. Possessive Pronouns

Do you want to borrow $\boxed{\text{my}}$ English book?
Do you want to borrow $\boxed{\text{mine?}}$

possessive adjective + noun	possessive pronoun
my book	mine
your book	yours
his book	his
her book	hers
their book	theirs

PRACTICE

Circle the correct word.

1. ■ Can I borrow (your) / yours English book?

   ☐ Why don't you ask Oscar and Gloria?

2. ■ I did. They didn't bring their / theirs today.

   ☐ How about Julia?

3. ■ I can't borrow her / hers book. She's in my / mine class.

4. ☐ What happened to your / yours English book?

   ■ I lost it.

5. ☐ Well, I guess you can borrow my / mine , but I want it back.

6. ■ O. K. Wait a minute. This book looks like my / mine . It has

   my / mine name on it.

7. ☐ If that's your / yours book, then where's my / mine ?

8. ■ I don't know. I guess you lost your / yours. Do you want to

   borrow my / mine ?

MAKE IT WORK

Fill in the dialogue with *my* or *mine*.

■ Is that _____ coat?

☐ No. It's _____.

■ It looks just like _____ coat.

HE SPILLED COFFEE ALL OVER HIS FAVORITE SUIT.

Regular and Irregular Past Tense Verbs

PRACTICE

Fill in the blanks with the correct past tense form.

1. (get) Michael _got_____ up at 8:30 last Tuesday.
2. (be) He _____ late for work.
3. (shave) (not/be) First, he _____, but he
    _____ very careful.
4. (cut) He _____ his face.
5. (take) Then he _____ a shower.
6. (not/be) There _____ any hot water.
7. (have) He _____ to take a cold shower.
8. (go) After his shower he _____ into the bedroom.
9. (decide) He _____ to wear his favorite suit.
10. (put) He _____ it on.
11. (go) Then he _____ into the kitchen.
12. (read) (eat) He _____ the newspaper, and he
    _____ breakfast.
13. (drink) He _____ some coffee with his breakfast.
14. (spill) Then he _____ coffee all over his
    favorite suit.
15. (be) It _____ a terrible day!

MAKE IT WORK

Tell about a terrible day you had.

Were you in a hurry? Did you hurt yourself? Did you fall down? Did you spill
anything? Did you miss your train, bus, or subway?

_____

_____

_____

_____

HIS DREAM CAME TRUE.

Regular and Irregular Past Tense Verbs

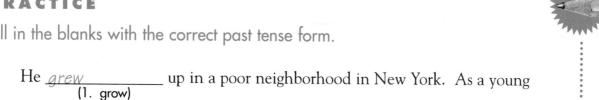

His dream came true.

Note: irregular past tense verbs:

come → came   grow → grew

become → became   sleep → slept

sell → sold

PRACTICE

Fill in the blanks with the correct past tense form.

He _grew_ (1. grow) up in a poor neighborhood in New York. As a young

actor, he _____ (2. make) no money. He _____ (3. live) on $30.00 a week.

At night he sometimes _____ (4. sleep) in the park.

He _____ (5. want) to be a famous actor, but he couldn't get a job. He

_____ (6. decide) to write his own movie script and act in the movie.

In 1974 he _____ (7. write) a movie script. He _____ (8. take) it to

every movie company in Hollywood. At that time, he _____ (9. have) only

$106.00 in the bank. But he still _____ (10. refuse) $300,000 for his script

because he wanted to act in the movie as well.

Finally, his dream _____ (11. come) true. He _____ (12. sell) the script

and _____ (13. become) a famous actor. He _____ (14. earn) $2 million from the

film *Rocky*. Today Sylvester Stallone has $40 million in the bank.

THE GIANTS WON.

Regular and Irregular Past Tense Verbs

SCORE	The score	was	3 to 2.
Braves 2	The Giants	won.	
Giants 3	The Braves	lost.	

Note: irregular past tense verbs:
win → won   hit → hit   beat → beat   shoot → shot

PRACTICE

Fill in the blanks with the correct past tense form.

I'm Bud Ortega with today's sports. Good evening, folks. Tonight in

baseball, the Atlanta Braves _played_ the San Francisco Giants. Rusty
(1. play)

Brown _____ a home run, and the Giants _____. The
(2. hit)   (3. win)

score _____ 3 to 2. In tennis, Mike Wong _____ Henry
(4. be)   (5. defeat)

Waterson in a very close match. Wong _____ Waterson 6–5, 6–5,
(6. beat)

6–4. At the PGA Golf Classic, Bob Blake _____ a score of 266 and
(7. shoot)

_____ first. He _____ by three points. In basketball, the
(8. finish)   (9. win)

Lakers _____ the Chicago Bulls in Los Angeles. Doug Washington
(10. play)

of the Bulls _____ the best player with 26 points. The Lakers
(11. be)

_____, 95 to 97. In college football, it was Notre Dame against
(12. lose)

Princeton. The score _____ tied 14 to 14. And that's it in sports.
(13. be)

I'm Bud Ortega, reporting.

New Word: match = game

WHO WON?

Subject and Object Questions

Regular and Irregular Past Tense Verbs

	subject	verb	object
	Who	won?	
The	Giants	won.	
Who did	they	play?	
	They	played	the Braves.

Note: Subject questions follow statement word order.

PRACTICE

Make questions.

1. ☐ San Francisco played St. Louis tonight.

   ◼ *Who won?* _____

   ☐ San Francisco.

   ◼ *What was the score?* _____

   ☐ 6 to 3.

2. ☐ José Garcia lost his tennis match yesterday.

   ◼ _____

   ☐ He played Mike Wong.

   ◼ _____

   ☐ 6–2, 6–4, 6–0.

3. ☐ The Celtics won again tonight.

   ◼ _____

   ☐ They played the Knicks.

   ◼ _____

   ☐ 110 to 90.

4. ☐ I went to the Raiders and the Broncos game last night.

   ◼ _____

   ☐ The Raiders.

   ◼ _____

   ☐ 7 to 0.

5. ☐ Did you see the tennis matches on TV? Christa Muller played a great match.

   ■ _____

   ☐ Ann Jackson.

   ■ _____

   ☐ Christa won. The score was 6–1, 6–4.

6. ■ I didn't see the ice hockey game. _____

   ☐ The Mighty Ducks won.

   ■ _____

   ☐ It was 3 to 1.

7. ☐ I saw the Golf Championship on TV yesterday.

   ■ _____

   ☐ Bob Blake won.

8. ☐ Did you see the soccer game?

   ■ No. _____

   ☐ Italy won.

   ■ _____

   ☐ They played Brazil.

   ■ _____

   ☐ 5 to 3.

9. ☐ The Knicks won again.

   ■ _____

   ☐ 97 to 95.

   ■ _____

   ☐ They played the Bulls.

10. ■ I didn't see the Giants game. _____

   ☐ The Giants won.

   ■ _____

   ☐ It was 3 to 2.

HE DIDN'T PARK BETWEEN THE LINES.

Negative Statements

Regular and Irregular Past Tense Verbs

She parked between the lines.

He didn't park between the lines.

contraction: didn't = did not

PRACTICE

Make negative sentences about *the man* in the picture above.

1. She parked close to the curb.   *He didn't park close to the curb.*

2. She turned off the motor.   _____

3. She applied the parking brake.   _____
   _____

4. She shifted the car into park.   _____
   _____

5. She turned off the lights.   _____
   _____

6. She closed the windows.   _____

7. She turned off the radio.   _____
   _____

8. She took her keys with her.   _____
   _____

9. She locked the doors.   _____

10. She put money in the   _____
    parking meter.   _____

New Words: shift   curb   parking meter

HE DIDN'T SIGN THE REPORT.

Negative and Affirmative Statements

Regular and Irregular Past Tense Verbs

| He | got | the Norco report from Sandy. |
| He | didn't sign | the report. |

PRACTICE

Look at Jack Ripley's list of things to do. Then make negative or affirmative sentences. The items that have a check (✓) are things Jack Ripley did yesterday.

Jack Ripley's List of Things To Do

✓ get the Norco report from Sandy	talk to the accountant
look over the Norco report	✓ sign the checks
sign the report	write a letter to ABC Company
call Mark Gunn	order paper
✓ meet with Norco	send the Norco report to Mark Gunn
✓ have lunch with Art Jones	✓ leave early – appointment with Dr. Lau

---

1. _He got the Norco report from Sandy._
2. _____
3. _____
4. _____
5. _____
6. _____
7. _____
8. _____
9. _____
10. _____
11. _____
12. _____

MAKE IT WORK

Name one thing you didn't do yesterday.

_____

LAST FEBRUARY THEY FOUND A WALLET.

Negative and Affirmative Statements
Regular and Irregular Past Tense Verbs

Last February they | found | a wallet.

They | didn't keep | the wallet.

irregular past tense verbs: quit → quit
do → did
know → knew

PRACTICE

Fill in the blanks with the correct past tense form.

Tom and Pauline North _proved_____ that honesty pays. Last
       (1. prove)

February the Norths _____ a wallet with $2,394.00 in a mall in
                        (2. find)

El Paso, Texas. They _____ the wallet. They
                        (3. not/keep)

_____ it to the police station.
(4. take)

"We _____ to return the money. There
        (5. have)

_____ any question. The money _____ ours,"
   (6. not/be)   (7. not/be)

said Pauline North.

But Pauline, age 46, and Tom North, 44, are unemployed. Pauline

_____ her job last month. Two years ago her husband, Tom,
   (8. lose)

_____ his job as a printer because of health problems. Just
   (9. quit)

weeks before, they _____ a place to live, and they
                        (10. not/have)

_____ any money.
   (11. not/have)

LAST FEBRUARY THEY FOUND A WALLET.

The television and the newspapers _____ the North's story
(12. report)

last Friday. On Saturday they _____ hundreds of telephone
(13. receive)

calls from people all around the United States. Some people

_____ money. One person even _____ a check
(14. send)   (15. write)

for $2,400.00. Some people _____ bags of groceries for the
(16. leave)

Norths. Several people _____ Pauline North a job. A real
(17. offer)

estate agent _____ the Norths a free apartment for six months.
(18. give)

The Norths _____ more than 500 letters and $10,000.
(19. get)

They even _____ on a TV interview show. Pauline North
(20. appear)

_____, "I'm really surprised about all of this. We just
(21. say)

_____ the right thing."
(22. do)

MAKE IT WORK

Answer the questions about the story.

Did honesty "pay" for the Norths? _____

_____

What happened after television and newspapers reported the North's story?

_____

_____

_____

_____

_____

New Words: honesty = truthful, fair actions
unemployed = not working
quit = leave a job
free = not costing anything

THE PEOPLE IN THE STUDY DIDN'T EAT A LOT OF SALT.

Review: Simple Past

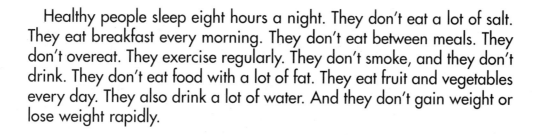

PRACTICE

Read the sentences. Then tell what 7,000 people in a study did in order to stay healthy. Change the present tense to past tense.

Healthy people sleep eight hours a night. They don't eat a lot of salt. They eat breakfast every morning. They don't eat between meals. They don't overeat. They exercise regularly. They don't smoke, and they don't drink. They don't eat food with a lot of fat. They eat fruit and vegetables every day. They also drink a lot of water. And they don't gain weight or lose weight rapidly.

The people in the study slept eight hours a night.

_____

_____

_____

_____

_____

_____

_____

_____

_____

_____

New Words: overeat = eat too much
gain = increase

MY OLD CAR WAS LUXURIOUS.

Contrast: Past vs. Present

My old car was luxurious.	My new car isn't luxurious.
My old car had leather seats.	My new car doesn't have leather seats.

PRACTICE

Fill in the blanks with the correct verb tense. Read the entire story before you begin.

I _bought_ a used car several years ago, but it
   (1. buy)

_____ an ordinary used car. It _____ a
   (2. not/be)   (3. be)

Mercedes Benz. It was six years old when I bought it, so it wasn't very

expensive. It _____ a luxurious car. It _____
   (4. be)   (5. have)

leather seats. It _____ smoothly. Even the radio
   (6. drive)

_____ excellent. People _____ my beautiful car.
   (7. be)   (8. admire)

They _____ my car was very expensive.
   (9. think)

    Last year I _____ the Mercedes Benz. Now I
             (10. sell)

_____ a new car. My new car _____ luxurious.
   (11. have)   (12. not/be)

It _____ leather seats. It _____ smoothly. And
   (13. not/have)   (14. not/drive)

my friends _____ my car.
   (15. not/admire)

MAKE IT WORK

Tell about something you bought and sold.

I bought _____

_____

Last year I sold _____ . Now _____

_____

SHE WANTS TO TAKE SOME ENGLISH CLASSES.

Contrast: Verb Forms

She		worked	in a hospital at first.
She		works	in a doctor's office now.
She	didn't	study	nursing at first.
She	doesn't	study	nursing now.
She	can't	study	nursing now.
She	will	study	nursing in the future.
She		wants	to take	some English classes.
She		needs	to take	some English classes.

PRACTICE

Fill in the blanks with the correct form of the verb. Read the entire story before you begin.

In her country Ann Tran was a nurse. She _arrived_ in the
(1. arrive)

United States two years ago. At first she didn't _____ English,
(2. speak)

so she _____ English for a year. Then she
(3. study)

_____ a job in a hospital as a nurse's aide. She
(4. get)

_____ jobs because she didn't want _____ at
(5. change) (6. work)

night.

She _____ a better job now. She _____ in
(7. have) (8. work)

a doctor's office. She doesn't _____ at night, but she sometimes
(9. work)

_____ on Saturday. In a few months Ann will
(10. work)

_____ her job. She'll _____ back to school.
(11. quit) (12. go)

SHE WANTS TO TAKE SOME ENGLISH CLASSES.

She wants _____ nursing. She'd like _____
           (13. study)   (14. work)

in a hospital, but she doesn't want _____ a nurse's aide. She
                                     (15. be)

wants a job as a nurse.

She'd like _____ part time and go to school full time. She
           (16. work)

also needs _____ some English classes. She can't
           (17. take)

_____ a better job until she _____ English
(18. get)   (19. speak)

better. With a little hard work and some luck, Ann's dream will

_____ true.
(20. come)

MAKE IT WORK

Answer the questions.

What was your first job?

_____

What didn't you like about your first job?

_____

What job do you have now?

_____

Is it a better job than your first job? Why?

_____

What are your plans for the future?

_____

_____

What is your dream?

_____

_____

THEY SPEAK DIFFERENT LANGUAGES.

Contrast: Past vs. Present

> They speak different languages.
> They met last April.

PRACTICE

Fill in the blanks with the correct verb tense. Read the entire story before you begin.

Betty Simpson and Naheed Kilic _don't speak_ the same language. She
(1. not/speak)

_____ English, and he _____ Turkish. Betty is a
(2. speak)   (3. speak)

nineteen-year-old from Las Vegas, Nevada. She _____ Naheed at a
(4. meet)

boxing match last April. Naheed, an eighteen-year-old boxer from Turkey,

_____ in the United States for the boxing match.
(5. be)

It all started when Naheed _____ the match. Betty was
(6. lose)

working at the boxing event. She _____ sorry for Naheed. She
(7. feel)

_____ up to him and _____. "When she smiled at me, I
(8. walk)   (9. smile)

_____ she _____ the woman for me," said Naheed.
(10. know)   (11. be)

Three weeks later, Naheed and Betty were married.

Today they _____ in Las Vegas, and Naheed _____
(12. live)   (13. take)

English lessons three times a week. Betty still _____ Turkish,
(14. not/speak)

and Naheed _____ English very well. But they
(15. not /speak)

_____ to each other three times a day with the help of an interpreter.
(16. talk)

New Word: interpreter = a person who translates for people who speak
different languages

123

Contrast: Past vs. Present

Profile of Dr. Allen Lau

Born:	April 11, 1953
Birthplace:	Taiwan
Residence:	Tustin, California
Education:	Samra University of Oriental Medicine, Los Angeles 1983–1985 Doctor of Philosophy degree, 1985
Profession:	doctor of acupuncture
Place of Employment:	the Eastern Medical Center I Tustin, California
Family:	wife, Cindy; son, Allen, Jr., age 3
Sports:	tennis, ping-pong
Hobbies:	collects antiques
Skills:	plays the piano
Languages:	Chinese, English
Goals:	To have three more children To buy a bigger house someday

New Word: acupuncture

HE WAS BORN IN TAIWAN. HE LIVES IN TUSTIN.

Contrast: Past vs. Present

Dr. Lau was born in Taiwan.

He came to the United States in 1983.

He lives in Tustin.

PRACTICE

Read the profile on page 124. Make affirmative sentences about Dr. Lau.

1. (born)   *Dr. Lau was born on April 11, 1953.*

2. (born) _____

3. (live) _____

4. (attend) _____

_____

5. (receive) _____

_____

6. (be) _____

7. (work) _____

_____

8. (be married) _____

9. (have) _____

10. (play) _____

11. (collect) _____

12. (play) _____

13. (speak) _____

14. (want) _____

15. (want) _____

MAKE IT WORK

Make one sentence about yourself for each category.

Education: _____

Goals: _____

_____

125

THE MAN NEXT DOOR WAS WATCHING TELEVISION.

Affirmative Statements

Past Continuous

> The man next door $\boxed{\text{was watching}}$ television.
> The man and woman next door $\boxed{\text{were watching}}$ television.
>
> Note: Use *was* or *were* + verb + *ing* to form the past continuous.
> Use the past continuous for an action that began before a second
> past action and continued up to or past the second action.
>
> continuing action: I was watching television from 9:30 to 11:30.
> second past action: Mrs. Rose's house was robbed at 10:34.

PRACTICE

Mrs. Rose's house was robbed at 10:34 A.M. yesterday. The police
questioned all the neighbors. Tell what each person was doing between 9:30
and 11:30 A.M. yesterday. Fill in the blanks with the correct verb form.

1. (watch)   The man next door _was watching_ television.

2. (play)   The two teenage boys next door _____
              ping-pong.

3. (work)   The woman and man across the street _____ in
              the backyard.

4. (take)   The woman down the street _____ a bath.

5. (shop)   The man up the street _____.

6. (listen)   The man and his son on the corner _____
              to a baseball game.

7. (study)   The children in back of her _____ .

8. (run)   The man in back of her _____ in the park.

9. (watch)   The babysitter across the street _____
              the children in the backyard.

10. (practice) The girl up the street _____ the piano.

MAKE IT WORK

Here is a description of the thief. Fill in the blanks.

He _was wearing_ a black leather jacket. He _____
a gun. He _____ a black 1990 Cadillac.

WHEN BOB CALLED ANDY, HE WAS STUDYING.

Affirmative Statements with _When_

Past Continuous

> | When | Bob called Andy, he | was studying. |
>
> | When | Bob called Susan and Bruce, they | were working | in the yard.
>
> Note: Use _when_ + the past continuous with an action that interrupted a continuing action in the past.

PRACTICE

Make sentences about Bob. Begin your sentences with _when_.

1. Andy/study   _When Bob called Andy, he was studying._

2. Brian/cook   _____

3. Linda/sleep   _____

4. Diane/iron   _____

5. Susan and Bruce/   _____
   work in the yard   _____

6. Barbara/wash her hair _____

7. Susan/water the plants _____

8. John/take a shower   _____

9. Dorothy and Leonard/ _____
   wash the car   _____

10. Carmen/practice the _____
    piano   _____

WAS HE DRIVING TOO FAST? YES, HE WAS.

Negative and Affirmative Short Answers

Past Continuous

Was he driving too slowly?	No, he wasn't.
Was he driving too fast?	Yes, he was.

PRACTICE

It was raining. John Burns was listening to the radio and singing along with the music. He was drinking soda. He was driving his car 70 miles an hour. The speed limit was 55 miles an hour, but he didn't see the sign because he wasn't wearing his glasses. A police officer stopped him.

Give short answers about John Burns.

1. Was it raining? _____Yes, it was._____

2. Was it snowing? _____

3. Was John listening to the radio? _____

4. Was he singing? _____

5. Was he paying attention? _____

6. Was he drinking soda? _____

7. Was he driving 55 miles an hour? _____

8. Was he driving 60 miles an hour? _____

9. Was he driving over 60 miles an hour? _____

10. Was he driving too slowly? _____

11. Was he speeding? _____

12. Was he wearing his glasses? _____

MAKE IT WORK

Answer John's questions.

Police Officer: May I see your driver's license?

John: Here, officer. Was I doing something wrong?

Police Officer: _____. You were speeding.

John: Was I driving over the speed limit?

Police Officer: _____. You were driving 70 miles an hour.

I'm going to give you a ticket.

THEY'RE MADE OF LEATHER.

Affirmative Statements

Be + Past Participle

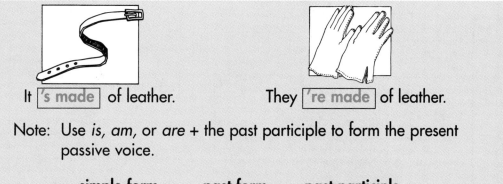

It 's made of leather.   They 're made of leather.

Note: Use *is, am,* or *are* + the past participle to form the present passive voice.

simple form	past form	past participle
make	made	made

PRACTICE

What are the following objects made of? Look at the pictures. Then make affirmative sentences.

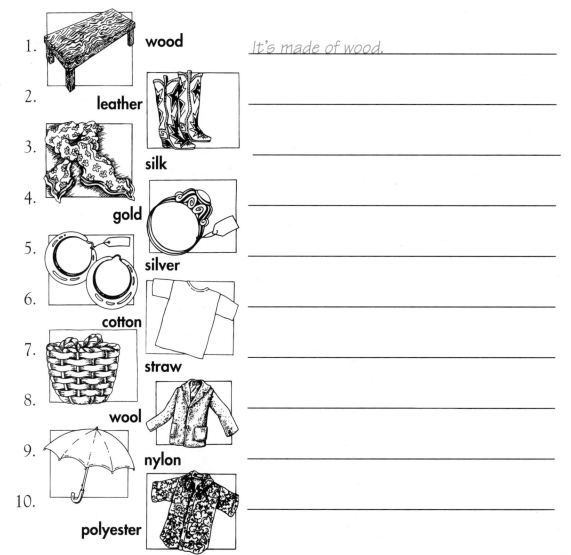

1. wood   *It's made of wood.* _____

2. leather   _____

3. silk   _____

4. gold   _____

5. silver   _____

6. cotton   _____

7. straw   _____

8. wool   _____

9. nylon   _____

10. polyester   _____

Negative and Affirmative Short Answers

Be + Past Participle

Dear Carmen,

I'm in Quito. Quito is the capital of Ecuador. It's located in the mountains. Quito is known for its beautiful churches and its art. A lot of wool blankets are made in Quito. Also, a lot of straw hats are made here. They're called Panama hats, but they're made in Ecuador, not Panama. They're sold at the market every Saturday. I bought you a hat!

See you soon.

Samantha

Quito

POSTAL

Mrs. Carmen Burns

177 West Drive Apartment 1A

Los Angeles, CA 90069

USA

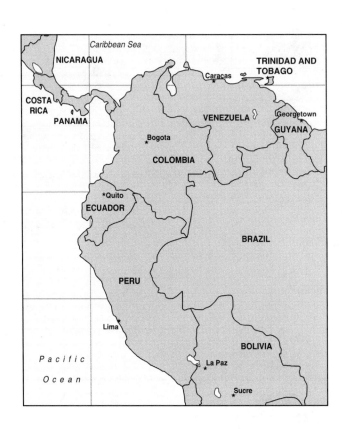

ARE BLANKETS MADE IN QUITO? YES, THEY ARE.

Is Quito known for its modern buildings?	No, it isn't.
Is Quito known for its beautiful churches?	Yes, it is.
Are silk scarves made in Quito?	No, they aren't.
Are blankets made in Quito?	Yes, they are.

Note: made **in** + Quito
          made **of** + wool

irregular past particles: know → known   make → made   sell → sold

PRACTICE

Read the postcard on page 130. Then answer the questions with short answers.

1. Is Quito the capital of Ecuador?   *Yes, it is.* _____

2. Is Quito located on an island?   _____

3. Is Quito located in the mountains?   _____

4. Is it known for its modern buildings?   _____

5. Is it known for its beautiful churches?   _____

6. Is it known for its art?   _____

7. Are a lot of blankets made in Quito?   _____

8. Are the blankets made of wool?   _____

9. Are a lot of hats made in Quito?   _____

10. Are the hats made of leather?   _____

11. Are they made of straw?   _____

12. Are they called Panama hats?   _____

13. Are they made in Panama?   _____

14. Are they sold in a big store?   _____

15. Are they sold at a market?   _____

MAKE IT WORK

Name something you learned about Quito.

_____

STOP SIGNS AREN'T PAINTED GREEN.

Negative and Affirmative Statements

Be + Past Participle

> Stop signs aren't painted green.   They 're painted red.
> irregular past participles: wear → worn   write → written

PRACTICE

Correct the sentences below. First write a negative sentence; then write an affirmative sentence.

Comb is spelled with a *k*.

1. *Comb isn't spelled with a k.*

2. *It's spelled with a c.*

Soup is eaten with a fork.

3. _____

4. _____

Chopsticks are used in Brazil.

5. _____

6. _____

Juice is served hot.

7. _____

8. _____

Medicine is sold in a department store.

9. _____

10. _____

Rings are worn on your arms.

11. _____

12. _____

The word *french* is written with a small *f*.

13. _____

14. _____

New Word: chopsticks

132

WHAT'S MADE IN FRANCE?

Questions with *What*

***Be* + Past Participle**

What language	is spoken in France?	French
What	's grown in France?	Grapes
What	's made in France?	Wine

contraction: what's = what is
irregular past participles: grow → grown   speak → spoken

PRACTICE

Ask three questions about each country. Begin your sentences with *what.*

Cuba

1. _What language is spoken in Cuba?_____ Spanish

2. _____ Sugar

3. _____ Cigars

Italy

4. _____ Olives

5. _____ Olive Oil

6. _____ Italian

Brazil

7. _____ Portuguese

8. _____ Coffee beans

9. _____ Coffee

Japan

10. _____ Cars and Cameras

11. _____ Rice

12. _____ Japanese

MAKE IT WORK

Complete the dialogue.

■ Where are you from?   ■ _____ ?

☐ Canada.   ☐ English and French.

133

SILVER JEWELRY IS MADE IN MEXICO.

Review: *Be* **+ Past Participle**

> Rosa is from Mexico.
>
> Spanish | is spoken | in Mexico.
>
> Corn | is grown | in Mexico.
>
> Silver jewelry | is made | in Mexico.

PRACTICE

Interview three classmates using the questions on page 133. Then tell about three of your classmates' home countries.

1. _____
   _____
   _____
   _____

2. _____
   _____
   _____
   _____

3. _____
   _____
   _____
   _____

MAKE IT WORK

Answer the questions.

What language is spoken in your country?

_____

What's made in your country?

_____

What's grown in your country?

_____

ANSWERS TO EXERCISES

Page 1
2. aren't, They're
3. isn't, He's
4. aren't. They're
5. isn't, She's
6. aren't, They're
7. isn't, She's
8. aren't, They're
9. isn't, He's
10. isn't, She's
11. aren't, They're
12. isn't, He's

Page 2
2. Whose gloves are they?
3. Whose wallet is it?
4. Whose keys are they?
5. Whose books are they?
6. Whose scarf is it?
7. Whose credit cards are they?
8. Whose pens are they?
9. Whose camera is it?
10. Whose pencils are they?
11. Whose coat is it?
12. Whose papers are they?
13. Whose purse is it?
14. Whose hat is it?

Make It Work
Are these your glasses?
No, they aren't.
Then whose glasses are they?
I don't know.

Page 3
2. It's the waitress's pencil.
3. They're Gloria's keys.
4. It's Robert's wallet.
5. It's the boss's office.
6. It's Anita's scarf.
7. They're Mark Gunn's sunglasses.
8. They're Dr. Adams's gloves.
9. It's John Goode's camera.
10. They're Mr. Jones's books.
11. They're Dr. Bittel's glasses.
12. It's Brian Burns's business card.
13. It's Charles's coat.
14. They're Dr. Morgan's papers.
Note: When a singular noun ends in s, it is correct to add either 's or to use the apostrophe alone.

Pages 4 and 5
2. It's on the second floor.
3. It's on the tenth floor.
4. They're on the first floor.
5. It's on the fifth floor.
6. It's on the seventh floor.
7. They're on the tenth floor.
8. It's on the third floor.
9. It's on the eighth floor.
10. It's on the ninth floor.
11. They're on the first floor.
12. It's on the fourth floor.
13. It's on the sixth floor.
14. They're on the first floor.

Page 6
2. They're in the girls' department.
3. They're in the men's department.
4. They're in the women's department.
5. They're in the boy's department.
6. They're in the children's department.
7. They're in the girls' department.
8. They're in the ladies' department.
9. They're in the men's department.
10. They're in the children's department.
11. They're in the boys' department.
12. They're in the women's department.

Make It Work
They're in the children's department.

Page 7
2. on
3. in
4. in
5. on
6. in
7. on
8. on
9. in
10. on
11. in
12. in
13. on

Page 8
2. in
3. on
4. on
5. in
6. in
7. on
8. on, in
9. in
10. on
11. in
12. on
13. on
14. in
15. on

Pages 9 and 10
2. When is it open?
It's open from 6 A. M. to 4:30 P. M.
3. When is it closed?
It's closed on Mondays.
4. Where is it?
It's in the Towers Building on the tenth floor.
5. What kind of restaurant is Wong's?   It's Chinese.
6. When is it open?
It's open from 12:30 to 10:00 P. M.
7. When is it closed?
It's closed in August.
8. Where is it?
It's on Harbor Boulevard near Disneyland.
9. What kind of restaurant is Bob's?
It's Mexican.
10. When is it open?
It's open (every day) from 10:00 A. M. to 12:00 P. M.
11. When it is closed?
It's closed on December 25th.
12. Where is it?
It's in the Tishman Building (in Orange).
13. What kind of restaurant is Pierre's?
It's French.
14. When is it open?
It's open from 6 P. M. to 9:30 P. M. (Monday through Saturday).
15. When is it closed?
It's closed on Sunday(s).

16. Where is it?
    It's in the Newport Building on the top floor (in Newport Beach).

Page 11

2. Where's Connie Rivera's apartment?
   It's on the third floor.
3. Where's Anita Hug's apartment?
   It's on the second floor.
4. Where's Art Jones's apartment?
   It's on the second floor.
5. Where's Samantha Porter's apartment?
   It's on the first floor.
6. Where's Brian and Carmen Burns's (Burns') apartment?
   It's on the first floor.
7. Where's the superintendent's apartment?
   It's in the basement.

Make It Work

's, in, on, th

Pages 12 and 13

2. There isn't a laundromat on Green Street.
3. There's a bus stop on Green Street.
4. There are trees on Green Street.
5. There's an apartment building on Green Street.
6. There aren't (any) street lights on Green Street.
7. There's a drugstore on Green Street.
8. There's a gas station on Green Street.
9. There are two mailboxes on Green Street.
10. There are sidewalks on Green Street.
11. There isn't a fire hydrant on Green Street.
12. There's a grocery store on Green Street.
13. There isn't a parking lot on Green Street.
14. There isn't a park on Green Street.

Page 14

2. Are there
3. Is there
4. Are there
5. Is there
6. Are there
7. Is there
8. Are there
9. Is there
10. Are there
11. Is there
12. Are there
13. Is there
14. Is there

Make It Work

Is there a bus stop (fire hydrant) on Green Street?
Are there mailboxes on Green Street?

Page 15

2. There's some pepper in the cabinet.
3. There are some onions in the cabinet.
4. There are some potatoes in the cabinet.
5. There's some flour in the cabinet.
6. There's some sugar in the cabinet.
7. There are some cookies in the cabinet.
8. There's some rice in the cabinet.
9. There's some tea in the cabinet.
10. There are some crackers in the cabinet.
11. There's some oil in the cabinet.
12. There's some coffee in the cabinet.

Page 16

2. There isn't any left.
3. There aren't any left.
4. There aren't any left.
5. There isn't any left.
6. There isn't any left.
7. There aren't any left.
8. There isn't any left.
9. There isn't any left.
10. There aren't any left.

Make It Work

There isn't any (left).
There aren't any

Page 17

2. There aren't any pens in Gloria's purse.
3. There's some makeup in Gloria's purse.
4. There are some tissues in Gloria's purse.
5. There isn't any medicine in Gloria's purse.
6. There's some gum in Gloria's purse.
7. There aren't any sunglasses in Gloria's purse.
8. There aren't any credit cards in Gloria's purse.
9. There are some keys in Gloria's purse.
10. There are some combs in Gloria's purse.
11. There's some candy in Gloria's purse.
12. There aren't any business cards in Gloria's purse.

Make It Work

Some possible answers are:
There are some pictures in my wallet.
There are some credit cards in my wallet.
There's some money in my wallet.

Page 18

2. How much cheese is there?
3. How many eggs are there?
4. How much orange juice is there?
5. How many apples are there?
6. How much steak is there?
7. How many strawberries are there?
8. How many potatoes are there?
9. How much lettuce is there?
10. How many cookies are there?
11. How much oil is there?
12. How much chicken is there?
13. How many tomatoes are there?
14. How much bread is there?

Page 19

2. All right, but just a little.
3. All right, but just a few.
4. All right, but just a little.
5. All right, but just a few.
6. All right, but just a little.
7. All right, but just a few.
8. All right, but just a little.
9. All right, but just a little.
10. All right, but just a few.
11. All right, but just a little.
12. All right, but just a few.
13. All right, but just a little.
14. All right, but just a few.

Make It Work
Some possible answers are:
All right, but just a little.
No, thank you.
Yes, please.

Page 20 and 21

2. bottles (cans) of
3. cans of
4. bags of
5. jar of
6. quarts of
7. loaves of
8. pounds of
9. heads of
10. bottles of
11. pounds of
12. dozen
13. bottle of
14. jar of
15. cans of

Page 22

2. Two cups of coffee, please.
3. Two glasses of soda, please.
4. Two pieces of chocolate cake, please.
5. Two bowls of vegetable soup, please.
6. Two glasses of water, please.
7. Two dishes of vanilla ice cream, please.
8. Two pieces of apple pie, please.
9. Two glasses of milk, please.
10. Two slices of pizza, please.
11. Two bowls of cereal, please.
12. Two cups of tea, please.

Make It Work
Two hamburgers, two pieces of apple pie, two cups of coffee, and one bowl of vegetable soup.

Page 23

2. 2 pounds of hamburger meat
3. 1 cup of Parmesan cheese
4. 2 onions
5. 1 cup of wine
6. 4 slices of bread
7. 4 eggs
8. 1/2 pound of butter
9. 1/3 cup of flour
10. 1 quart of milk
11. 2 cups of cottage cheese

Page 24

2. there's something
3. There isn't anything
4. there's something
5. There's something
6. there isn't anything
7. There isn't anything
8. there's something
9. There isn't anything
10. there's something

Pages 25

2. there's no one
3. There's no one
4. there's someone
5. There's someone
6. there's no one
7. There's someone
8. there's no one

Page 26

2. Yes, but she's sleeping now.
3. Yes, but he's taking a shower now.
4. Yes, but she's washing her hair now.
5. Yes, but they're eating dinner now.
6. Yes, but she's watching the baby now.
7. Yes, but he's studying now.
8. Yes, but they're working in the yard now.
9. Yes, but she's ironing now.
10. Yes, but she's watering the plants now.
11. Yes, but she's practicing the piano now.
12. Yes, but they're washing the car now.

Page 27

2. ning
3. ing
4. ping
5. ing
6. ing
7. ing (smiling)
8. ing
9. ing
10. ing (taking)
11. ing
12. ing
13. ing
14. ting
15. ing

Page 28

2. in
3. in
4. next to
5. next to
6. between
7. in front of
8. behind

Page 29

2. you're looking at me.
3. we're looking at him.
4. she's looking at them.
5. they're watching us.
6. you're watching her.
7. I'm watching him.
8. we're talking to you.
9. he's talking to me.
10. she's talking to them.
11. they're listening to us.
12. I'm listening to her.

Make It Work
her, her, him

Pages 30 and 31

2. is sitting in the tree.
3. is running toward(s) the tree.
4. is sitting near the tree.
5. is running up the tree.
6. is flying away from the tree.
7. is running down the tree.
8. is running around the tree.
9. is sitting on the cage.
10. is running toward(s) the cage.
11. is flying away from the cage.
12. is sitting in the cage.

Pages 32 and 33

2. The president and the first lady are getting out of the plane now.

3. The president is smiling and waving at the people.
4. Now the president and the first lady are walking down the stairs.
5. The president and the king are shaking hands.
6. The first lady is talking to the queen, and the queen is smiling.
7. The queen is wearing a suit, and the first lady is wearing a dress.
8. The king and the president are getting into a limousine.
9. The first lady and the queen are getting into a limousine.
10. The people are waving and shouting.

Page 34
2. isn't standing
3. are standing
4. aren't looking
5. 're looking
6. aren't holding
7. 're holding
8. aren't kissing
9. 're cutting
10. isn't wearing
11. 's wearing
12. is wearing
13. 's smiling
14. isn't smiling

Page 35
2. What's he frowning at?
3. What are they laughing at?
4. Who's she yelling at?
5. Who are you smiling at?
6. Who are they listening to?
7. Who's he waving at?
8. What are you looking at?
9. Who are you laughing at?
10. What are they clapping at?
11. Who's she talking to?
12. What's he listening to?

Make It Work
Who's she talking to?
What's she laughing at?

Page 36
2. 's talking
3. are standing (waiting)
4. 're waiting

5. 's (is) reading
6. is yelling (shouting)
7. is looking
8. is holding
9. 's (is) crying
10. aren't smiling (are angry/are frowning).

Page 37
2. is going to go
3. are going to watch
4. is going to stay
5. are going to have
6. are going to go
7. is going to take
8. are going to go
9. are going to have
10. is going to visit
11. are going to work
12. is going to go

Page 38
2. , so she's going to drink some water.
3. , so he's going to go to the dentist.
4. , so I'm going to visit some friends.
5. , so he's going to go to bed.
6. , so she's going to put on a sweater.
7. , so they're going to get some help.
8. , so I'm going to see a doctor.
9. , so she's going to ask for directions.
10. , so we're going to watch television.

Page 39
They aren't going to be married in a big church. They aren't going to invite a lot of people to their wedding. Sonia isn't going to wear a wedding dress. She isn't going to carry flowers. Peter isn't going to wear a tuxedo. Sonia and Peter aren't going to have a big reception after the wedding. They aren't going to have a cake, and they aren't going to serve champagne. They aren't going to have a band. Afterward they aren't going to go on a honeymoon.

Page 40
2. (What) kind of party is it going to be?
3. (What) time is it going to start?
4. (What) time is it going to end?
5. (Where) is it going to be?
6. (Where) is it going to be?
7. (When) is it going to be?
8. (What) are they going to bring?
9. (What) are they going to wear?
10. (What) is (What's) her telephone number?

Page 41
2. will go, 'll study
3. will travel, 'll visit
4. will look
5. will take
6. will get married
7. will get
8. will work, 'll study
9. will return, 'll work
10. 'll ask

Page 42
2. will meet ('ll meet)
3. will be ('ll be)
4. will fall ('ll fall)
5. will marry ('ll marry)
6. will have
7. will be
8. will have ('ll have)
9. will move
10. will live ('ll live)
11. will be
12. will get
13. will have ('ll have)
14. will live ('ll live)
15. will be ('ll be)

Page 43
Individual answers. Some possible answers are:
2. Will my husband be successful?
3. Will my children go to college?
4. Will my children get married (divorced)?
5. Will my children be famous?
6. Will my children have a lot of children?

7. Will I be rich (happy)?
8. Will I win the lottery?
9. Will I have a long life?
10. Will I have a lot of money?
11. Will I be healthy?
12. Will my wife change jobs?

Page 44

2. No, she won't.
3. No, she won't.
4. Yes, he will.
5. No, he won't.
6. Yes, he will.
7. Yes, she will.
8. No, she won't.
9. No, they won't.
10. Yes, they will.
11. No, they won't.
12. Yes, they will.

Make It Work

Yes, I will. (No, I won't.)

Page 45

2. She won't hang up her clothes.
3. They won't make their beds.
4. He won't take out the trash.
5. They won't eat vegetables.
6. She won't wash the dishes.
7. He won't walk the dog.
8. She won't feed the dog.
9. He won't get a part-time job.
10. They won't help around the house.
11. She won't practice the piano.
12. He won't mow the lawn.

Page 46

Individual answers.
(I'll.... / I won't....)

Page 47

Individual answers.

Page 48

2. I collect stamps.
3. We collect coins.
4. She collects dolls.
5. They collect buttons.
6. He collects baseball cards.
7. I collect antiques.
8. She collects matchbooks.
9. He collects postcards.
10. They collect old records.

Make It Work

Individual answers.

Page 49

2. (She) doesn't commute three hours a day.
3. She doesn't take the train.
4. She doesn't get up at 5:30.
5. She doesn't drive to the train station.
6. She doesn't wait for the train.
7. She doesn't arrive in New York at 8:00.
8. She doesn't take a bus.
9. She doesn't walk to her office.
10. She doesn't arrive at her office late.

Page 50

2. They don't get up early.
3. They don't have a quick breakfast.
4. (Gloria) doesn't take the bus to work.
5. She doesn't arrive at work at 9:00.
6. She doesn't decorate people's houses all day.
7. (Oscar) doesn't drive to work.
8. He doesn't work from 8:00 to 5:00.
9. He doesn't work in a dentist's office.
10. He doesn't see patients all day.
11. He doesn't get home at 6:00.
12. He doesn't fix dinner.
13. (Gloria) doesn't get home at 7:00.
14. They don't go to bed early.

Page 51

Individual answers.
(I like... /I don't like....)

Page 52

Individual answers. Some possible answers are:
I (don't) like to watch television (baseball games).
I (don't) like to go to parties.
(concerts/baseball games/ the movies).
I (don't) like to iron. (cook/read/listen to the radio/clean the house/ get up early).

Page 53

2. like
3. like
4. like to
5. likes to
6. likes
7. like
8. like to
9. likes
10. likes to
11. like
12. like to
13. likes
14. likes to
15. like to
16. like

Page 54

2. like to
3. want to
4. need
5. like to
6. like
7. like to
8. want to
9. like
10. like
11. want to
12. need to
13. like to

Page 55

2. I like the striped one.
3. I like the gray ones.
4. I like the white one.
5. I like the gold ones.
6. I like the gray one.
7. I like the white ones.
8. I like the black ones.
9. I like the plaid one.
10. I like the striped ones.
11. I like the gold one.
12. I like the black ones.
13. I like the plain one.
14. I like the white ones.

Page 56

2. Which one do you want?

3. Which ones do you want?
4. Which ones do you want?
5. Which one do you want?
6. Which one do you want?
7. Which one do you want?
8. Which one do you want?
9. Which one do you want?
10. Which ones do you want?
11. Which one do you want?
12. Which ones do you want?

Make It Work

I want the big (ger) one. (I want the one on the right.)

Page 57

Individual answers.

Page 58

2. Does he ever go
3. Do they ever read
4. Does she ever cook
5. Do they ever go
6. Does he ever wear
7. Do you ever play
8. Does she ever sleep
9. Do they ever work
10. Does he ever take
11. Do you ever drink
12. Does she ever go

Page 59

Individual answers.

Pages 60

2. How often do they exercise?
3. How often does he watch the news on TV?
4. How often do you read the newspaper?
5. How often does she visit her family?
6. How often do they go to concerts?
7. How often does he play chess?
8. How often do you go to the movies?
9. How often does she play tennis?
10. How often does she go to church?
11. How often do they eat out?
12. How often do you go to the beach?

Make It Work

How often do you eat?
How often do you go to Pierre's French Restaurant?

Page 61

2. I drive slowly.
3. He drives fast.
4. They learn quickly.
5. You learn slowly.
6. I write well.
7. She writes poorly.
8. We read quickly.
9. They read slowly.
10. He dances well.
11. She dances badly.
12. You work carefully.
13. We work hard.
14. He plays tennis well.
15. I play tennis badly.

Pages 62 and 63

2. He usually stays home.
3. He watches movies and talks to his son.
4. (Oscar Hernandez) works hard all week.
5. He doesn't like to stay home on Saturday night.
6. He needs to talk to people.
7. He wants to talk about his week.
8. (Anita Hug) never misses the dance at Leisure World.
9. She always has a ball.
10. (Linda Chan) likes to ride in her car with Pearl Jam on the radio.
11. She sometimes rents a video and eats popcorn.
12. (Samantha Porter) always has a date on Saturday night.
13. She needs to be with someone.
14. (Mark Gunn) doesn't plan his Saturday nights.
15. He goes to a bar or a party.
16. He always has fun.

Pages 64 and 65

2. I'm an architect.
3. I design buildings.
4. What do you do in your free time?

5. I don't have a lot of free time.
6. I take a class three nights a week.
7. What do you usually do on the weekend?
8. I work on Saturday morning.
9. I usually go to church on Sunday.
10. You're very busy.
11. Yes, I am.
12. Do you ever take a vacation?
13. I go to Hawaii once a year.
14. What do you want to do in the future?
15. I want to get married someday.
16. I want to have children.

Make It Work

Do you ever take a vacation?
Yes, but I don't usually take a very long vacation.

Pages 66, 67 and 68

2. She works for the city of Tokyo.
3. Mary Ellen Spear is an interior decorator.
4. She works for the city of Dallas (, Texas).
5. Keiko likes to eat soup, rice, fish, and vegetables.
6. She always drinks hot tea with every meal.
7. Mary Ellen likes to eat meat, potatoes, salad, and vegetables.
8. She drinks a cup of coffee after every meal.
9. Keiko collects stamps.
10. Mary Ellen doesn't have a hobby.
11. Keiko is single.
12. She doesn't have any children.
13. Mary Ellen is married.
14. She has two children.
15. Keiko plays golf.
16. Mary Ellen plays tennis.
17. Keiko wears suits at (to) work.
18. She doesn't wear any bright colors at (to) work.
19. Mary Ellen wears suits and dresses at (to) work.

20. She never wears pants at (to) work.
21. Keiko likes to watch television news shows.
22. Mary Ellen likes to go to (the) movies.
23. Keiko goes to Hawaii once a year.
24. Mary Ellen goes to Mexico every winter.

Page 69
Individual answers.

Page 70
3. and she is too.
4. and she does too.
5. and she is too.
6. and she is too.
7. and she does too.
8. and she does too.
9. and she is too.
10. and she is too.
11. and she is too.
12. and she does too.
13. and she does too.
14. and she does too.

Page 71
2. and he isn't either.
3. and he doesn't either.
4. and he isn't either.
5. and he doesn't either.
6. and he isn't either.
7. and he doesn't either.
8. and he doesn't either.
9. and he doesn't either.
10. and he doesn't either.
11. and he isn't either.
12. and he doesn't either.
13. and he isn't either.
14. and he doesn't either.

Page 72
2. but dogs are.
3. but dogs do.
4. but dogs aren't.
5. but dogs don't.
6. but dogs are.
7. but dogs do.
8. but dogs don't.
9. but dogs don't.
10. but dogs don't.
11. but dogs do.
12. but dogs don't.

13. but dogs don't.
14. but dogs don't.

Page 73
Individual answers.

Page 74
1. 'm decorating
2. 're, play, 're playing
3. writes, 's, 's writing
4. 's, paints, 's painting
5. 're, act, 're acting
6. 'm, 'm designing, design, design

Page 75
2. Do you have anything wider?
3. Do you have anything shorter?
4. Do you have anything longer?
5. Do you have anything smaller?
6. Do you have anything higher?
7. Do you have anything tighter?
8. Do you have anything larger?
9. Do you have anything sharper?
10. Do you have anything smaller?
11. Do you have anything looser?
12. Do you have anything cheaper?
13. Do you have anything wider?
14. Do you have anything lighter?
15. Do you have anything lower?

Pages 76
2. Susan is thinner than Joe.
3. Jenny is older than her sister.
4. Molly is heavier than Polly.
5. Paul is taller than Laura.
6. Ron is fatter than Ed.
7. Diane is prettier than her sister.
8. The secretary is smarter than her boss.

9. Philip is noisier than Dave.
10. Mike is messier than his secretary.

Page 77
2. more elegant than
3. more beautiful than
4. more powerful than
5. more economical than
6. more expensive than
7. more popular than
8. more practical than
9. more comfortable than
10. cheaper.

Page 78
2. older
3. more charming
4. cheaper
5. lower
6. bigger
7. smaller
8. larger
9. more expensive
10. more modern
11. smaller
12. larger
13. higher
14. more elegant
15. better

Page 79
2. Donna is the oldest.
3. Connie is the youngest.
4. Connie is the tallest.
5. Jean is the shortest.
6. Connie is the heaviest.
7. Jean is the lightest.
8. Jean is the prettiest.
9. Jean is the neatest.
10. Donna is the smartest.

Page 80
Individual answers ending with:
2. ...is the most exciting.
3. ...are the most intelligent.
4. ...is the most delicious.
5. ...is the most valuable.
6. ...are the most popular.
7. ...is the most practical.
8. ...are the most interesting.
9. ...are the most beautiful.
10. ...is the most famous.

Page 81
2. the oldest
3. the most modern
4. the busiest
5. the most important
6. the most popular
7. the richest
8. the largest
9. the longest
10. the most important
11. the best
12. the most beautiful

Page 82
Individual answers ending with:
2. ...is the most exciting.
3. ...is more expensive.
4. ...is a better singer.
5. ...is (are) the most popular.
6. ...are the most interesting.
7. ...is larger.
8. ...is the best actor.
9. ...are more beautiful.
10. ...is more popular.

Page 83
2. Cut off the ends of the beans.
3. Boil 2 cups of water.
4. Add the beans.
5. Cook them.
6. Drain the water off.
7. Put the beans on a plate.
8. Put butter on top.
9. Serve them.
Make It Work
1. Boil
2. Add
3. Cook
4. Drain
5. Serve

Page 84
2. Would you please close (it?)
3. Would you please turn (it off?)
4. Would you please answer (it?)
5. Would you please open (it?)
6. Would you please turn (it off?)
7. Would you please turn (it off?)
8. Would you please answer (the door?)
9. Would you please turn (it up?)
10. Would you please turn (it on?)
11. Would you please close (it?)
12. Would you please turn (the stove down?)
Make It Work
Would you please take (off your hat?)
Would you please sit (down?)
Would you please be (quiet?)

Page 85
2. May (Can) I speak to Dr. Lau?
3. May (Can) I come in?
4. Can (May) I use the (your) telephone?
5. May (Can) I leave early?
6. Can (May) I borrow a dollar?
7. May (Can) I ask (you) a question?
8. Can (May) I have a piece of paper?
9. Can (May) I use the (your) bathroom?
10. May (Can) I help you?

Page 86
2. Let's dance.
3. Let's eat out.
4. Let's go to the movies.
5. Let's listen to music.
6. Let's go to a soccer game.
7. Let's play cards.
8. Let's go to the park.
9. Let's play tennis.
10. Let's go to a concert.
11. Let's rent a video.
12. Let's take a walk.
13. Let's have a party.
14. Let's stay home.

Page 87
2. Let's go by plane.
3. Let's go by taxi.
4. Let's go by bus.
5. Let's go by plane.
6. Let's go by taxi.
7. Let's go by car.
8. Let's go by plane.
9. Let's go by train.
10. Let's go by subway.

Page 88
2. Let's not go by bus.
3. Let's not go by taxi.
4. Let's not go by train.
5. Let's not go by ferry.
6. Let's not go by boat.
7. Let's not go by train.
8. Let's not go by bus.
9. Let's not go by car.
10. Let's not go by plane.
11. Let's not go by subway.
12. Let's not go by bus.
Make It Work
Let's not go by taxi. It's too expensive.
Let's not go by bus. It's too slow (crowded).

Page 89
2. You shouldn't be late.
3. You should dress neatly.
4. You shouldn't wear flashy clothes.
5. You should speak clearly.
6. You shouldn't chew gum.
7. You should be polite.
8. You should look at the interviewer.
9. You should sit up straight.
10. You shouldn't smoke.
11. You should answer the interviewer's questions.
12. You should thank the interviewer for his or her time.
Make It Work
Possible answers:
He shouldn't smoke.
He should dress neatly.
He should wear a suit.
He shouldn't wear shorts and a T-shirt.
He should cut his hair.
He should tie his shoelaces.

Page 90
2. You can drive across the Golden Gate Bridge.
3. You can see Fisherman's Wharf.
4. You can eat fantastic seafood.
5. You can go to Chinatown.
6. You can take a boat tour of San Francisco Bay.

7. You can go to North Beach.
8. You can walk (take a walk) in Golden Gate Park.
9. You can visit the beautiful city of Carmel.
10. You can see the sea lions at Seal Rock.

Page 91
2. Where can you get a magazine?
   You can get a magazine at a newsstand (drugstore).
3. Where can you get some traveler's checks?
   You can get some traveler's checks at a bank.
4. Where can you get some medicine?
   You can get some medicine at a drugstore.
5. Where can you get some gum?
   You can get some gum at a drugstore (newsstand).
6. Where can you get a newspaper?
   You can get a newspaper at a newsstand (drugstore).
7. Where can you get a hamburger?
   You can get a hamburger at a coffee shop.
8. Where can you get some gasoline?
   You can get some gasoline at a gas station.

Page 92
2. You can't drink
3. You can't ride
4. You can't drink
5. You can't take (bring)
6. You can't walk

Pages 93
2. They'd like some help.
3. He'd like a sweater.
4. He'd like some food.
5. I'd like some rest.
6. They'd like some medicine.
7. He'd like some money.
8. They'd like a map.
9. We'd like some dry clothes.
10. She'd like some company.

Page 94
2. Would they like some cake?
3. Would you like a blanket?
4. Would she like some cold water?
5. Would you like some dry clothes?
6. Would you like a good book?
7. Would you like some coffee?
8. Would he like some medicine?
9. Would you like some directions?
10. Would he like some money?
11. Would they like some help?
12. Would she like some company?
13. Would he like some water?
14. Would you like a hamburger?
15. Would you like a map?

Make It Work
(Would you like) a cough drop?
Would you like some aspirin?
Would you like a bandage?

Page 95
2. Would you like to go skiing?
3. Would you like to go sailing?
4. Would you like to go swimming?
5. Would you like to go ice-skating?
6. Would you like to go horseback riding?
7. Would you like to go bowling?
8. Would you like to go camping?
9. Would you like to go jogging?
10. Would you like to go bicycle riding?

Make It Work
Would you like to go shopping (today)?

Page 96
2. He has to work.
3. I have to wash my hair.
4. You have to clean the house.
5. She has to wash her clothes.
6. He has to write some letters.

7. We have to visit our parents.
8. They have to go to a meeting.
9. He has to write a report.
10. I have to go to bed early.
11. She has to babysit.
12. They have to study.
13. You have to practice the piano.
14. I have to go to the doctor.

Make It Work
Possible answers:
Sorry, I can't. I have to (study, babysit, work).

Page 97
2. She doesn't have to go to bed early.
3. She doesn't have to go to work.
4. She doesn't have to be on time.
5. She doesn't have to cook.
6. She doesn't have to do the dishes.
7. She doesn't have to do her homework.
8. She doesn't have to clean the house.
9. She doesn't have to iron her clothes.
10. She doesn't have to wash her clothes.
11. She doesn't have to work in the yard.
12. She doesn't have to feed the cat.

Page 98
2. Does she have to have an interview?
3. Do you have to fill out an application?
4. Do you have to take a written test?
5. Do you have to take a driving test?
6. Do they have to deposit some money in the bank?
7. Do they have to fill out a form?
8. Do they have to sign their names?
9. Does he have to endorse the check?

10. Does he have to show his driver's license?

Pages 99 and 100
2. have to, can
3. have to, have to
4. have to, can, can't
5. have to, can
6. have to , can't
7. can't, have to
8. can't, have to
9. can, can't
10. can, have to

Pages 101 and 102
2. I'd like a cup of coffee (some coffee). (A cup of coffee, please. I want some coffee, please.)
3. Sorry. (I'd like to, but I can't.) I can't. I have to go to the doctor.
4. You should see a doctor. You shouldn't walk on it (your leg). (Don't move.)
5. Let's go to the early show. (Why don't we go to the early show?)
6. Would you like to go shopping Saturday? (Do you want to go shopping with me Saturday?)
7. Would you please sit down?
8. May (Can) I leave work early(this afternoon)? I have to go to the doctor.
9. Would you please turn the sound up?
10. I can buy a bag of potato chips and (a pack of) gum, or I can buy a candy bar.

Page 103
2. There were some gloves on the table a few minutes ago.
3. There were some keys on the table a few minutes ago.
4. There was a purse on the table a few minutes ago.
5. There were some glasses on the table a few minutes ago.
6. There was a checkbook on the table a few minutes ago.
7. There were some credit cards on the table a few minutes ago.

8. There was a wallet on the table a few minutes ago.
9. There was a camera on the table a few minutes ago.
10. There were some matches on the table a few minutes ago.

Make It Work
There were some credit cards on the table a few minutes ago.

Page 104
2. There weren't any food deliveries.
3. There weren't any mail deliveries.
4. There wasn't any telephone service.
5. There weren't any people on the street.
6. There wasn't any electricity.
7. There weren't any lights in the town.
8. There weren't any elevators working.
9. There wasn't any heat.
10. There wasn't any hot water.

Page 105
She fixed breakfast at 7:00. After breakfast she washed the dishes. Then she dried them. In the morning she cleaned the house. She vacuumed the rug, and she dusted the furniture. She emptied the wastepaper baskets. Then she carried out the trash. In the afternoon she washed the clothes. Then she folded them. She also changed the bed. Then she ironed. At 4:00 she shopped for food. And, of course, she cooked dinner at 6:00.

Page 106
Individual answers.

Page 107
Individual answers.

Page 108
2. (You) broke yours too.
3. (She) cut hers too.
4. (You) drove yours too.
5. (They) took theirs too.
6. (He) forgot his too.
7. (We) lost ours too.

8. (I) carried mine too.
9. (She) broke hers too.
10. (You) wore yours too.
11. (I) took mine too.
12. (They) lost theirs too.
13. (He) hurt his too.
14. (She) forgot hers too.
15. (We) paid ours too.
16. (I) cut mine too.

Page 109
2. theirs
3. her, my
4. your
5. mine
6. mine, my
7. your, mine
8. yours, mine

Make It Work
my, mine, my

Page 110
2. was
3. shaved, wasn't
4. cut
5. took
6. wasn't
7. had
8. went
9. decided
10. put
11. went
12. read, ate
13. drank
14. spilled
15. was

Page 111
2. made
3. lived
4. slept
5. wanted
6. decided
7. wrote
8. took
9. had
10. refused
11. came
12. sold
13. became
14. earned

Page 112
2. hit
3. won
4. was
5. defeated
6. beat
7. shot
8. finished
9. won
10. played

11. was
12. lost
13. was

Pages 113 and 114
2. Who did he play?
   What was the score?
3. Who did they play?
   What was the score?
4. Who won?
   What was the score?
5. Who did she play?
   Who won?
6. Who won?
   What was the score?
7. Who won?
8. Who won?
   Who did they play?
   What was the score?
9. What was the score?
   Who did they play?
10. Who won?
    What was the score?

Page 115
2. He didn't turn off the motor.
3. He didn't apply the parking brake.
4. He didn't shift the car into park.
5. He didn't turn off the lights.
6. He didn't close the windows.
7. He didn't turn off the radio.
8. He didn't take his keys with him.
9. He didn't lock the doors.
10. He didn't put money in the parking meter.

Page 116
2. He didn't look over the Norco report.
3. He didn't sign the report.
4. He didn't call Mark Gunn.
5. He met with Norco.
6. He had lunch with Art Jones.
7. He didn't talk to the accountant.
8. He signed the checks.
9. He didn't write a letter to ABC Company.
10. He didn't order paper.
11. He didn't send the Norco report to Mark Gunn.
12. He left early. (He had an appointment with Dr. Lau.)

Pages 117 and 118
2. found
3. didn't keep
4. took
5. had
6. wasn't
7. wasn't
8. lost
9. quit
10. didn't have
11. didn't have
12. reported
13. received
14. sent
15. wrote
16. left
17. offered
18. gave
19. got
20. appeared
21. said
22. did

Make It Work
Yes, it did.
They got over 500 letters and $10,000. They also got food and a free apartment. Pauline North got a job. The Norths also appeared on a television show.

Page 119
The didn't eat a lot of salt. They ate breakfast every morning. They didn't eat between meals. They didn't overeat. They exercised regularly. They didn't smoke, and they didn't drink. They didn't eat food with a lot of fat. They ate fruit and vegetables every day. They also drank a lot of water. And they didn't gain weight or lose weight.

Pages 120
2. wasn't
3. was
4. was
5. had
6. drove
7. was
8. admired
9. thought
10. sold
11. have
12. isn't
13. doesn't have
14. doesn't drive
15. don't admire

Pages 121 and 122
2. speak
3. studied
4. got
5. changed
6. to work

7. has
8. works
9. work
10. works
11. quit
12. go
13. to study
14. to work
15. to be
16. to work
17. to take
18. get
19. speaks
20. come

Page 123
2. speaks
3. speaks
4. met
5. was
6. lost
7. felt
8. walked
9. smiled
10. knew
11. was
12. live
13. takes
14. doesn't speak
15. doesn't speak
16. talk

Pages 124 and 125
2. He was born in Taiwan.
3. He lives in Tustin.
4. He attended Samra University of Oriental Medicine in Los Angeles (from 1983 to 1985).
5. He received a Doctor of Philosophy degree (in 1985).
6. He is a doctor of acupuncture.
7. He works at the Eastern Medical Center (in Tustin).
8. He's married (to Cindy).
9. He has a son (Allen).
10. He plays tennis and ping-pong.
11. He collects antiques. (His hobby is collecting antiques.)
12. He can play (plays) the piano.
13. He can speak (speaks) Chinese and English.

14. He want to have three more children.
15. He want to buy a bigger house someday.

Page 126
2. were playing
3. were working
4. was taking
5. was shopping
6. were listening
7. were studying
8. was running
9. was watching
10. was practicing
Make It Work
was carrying, was driving

Page 127
2. When Bob called Brian, he was cooking.
3. When Bob called Linda, she was sleeping.
4. When Bob called Diane, she was ironing.
5. When Bob called Susan and Bruce, they were working in the yard.
6. When Bob called Barbara, she was washing her hair.
7. When Bob called Susan, she was watering the plants.
8. When Bob called John, he was taking a shower.
9. When Bob called Dorothy and Leonard, they were washing the car.
10. When Bob called Carmen, she was practicing the piano.

Page 128
2. No, it wasn't.
3. Yes, he was.
4. Yes, he was.
5. No, he wasn't.
6. Yes, he was.
7. No, he wasn't.
8. No, he wasn't.
9. Yes, he was.
10. No, he wasn't.
11. Yes, he was.
12. No, he wasn't.
Make It Work
Yes, you were.
Yes, you were.

Page 129
2. They're made of leather.
3. It's made of silk.
4. It's made of gold.
5. They're made of silver.
6. It's made of cotton.
7. It's made of straw.
8. It's made of wool.
9. It's made of nylon.
10. It's made of polyester.

Pages 130 and 131
2. No, it isn't.
3. Yes, it is.
4. No, it isn't.
5. Yes, it is.
6. Yes, it is.
7. Yes, they are.
8. Yes, they are.
9. Yes, they are.
10. No, they aren't.
11. Yes, they are.
12. Yes, they are.
13. No, they aren't.
14. No, they aren't.
15. Yes, they are.

Page 132
3. Soup isn't eaten with a fork.
4. It's eaten with a spoon.
5. Chopsticks aren't used in Brazil.
6. They're used in Japan (China, Korea, Taiwan).
7. Juice isn't served hot.
8. It's served cold.
9. Medicine isn't sold in a department store.
10. It's sold in a drugstore.
11. Rings aren't worn on your arms.
12. They're worn on your fingers.
13. The word *French* isn't written with a small *f*.
14. It's written with a capital *F* (a large *F*).

Page 133
2. What's grown in Cuba?
3. What's made in Cuba?
4. What's grown in Italy?
5. What's made in Italy?
6. What language is spoken in Italy?
7. What language is spoken in Brazil?
8. What's grown in Brazil?
9. What's made in Brazil?
10. What's made in Japan?
11. What's grown in Japan?
12. What language is spoken in Japan?
Make It Work
What languages are spoken in Canada?

Page 134
Individual answers.